Edexcel GCSE

Business and Communication Systems

Sue Alpin ▪ Jan Cooper ▪ Fiona Petrucke ▪ Ged O'Hara

Hodder Arnold

A MEMBER OF THE HODDER HEADLINE GROUP

Orders: please contact Bookpoint Ltd, 130 Milton Park, Abingdon, Oxon OX14 4SB.
Telephone: (44) 01235 827720, Fax: (44) 01235 400454. Lines are open from
9.00 – 5.00, Monday to Saturday, with a 24 hour message answering service.
You can also order through our website: www.hoddereducation.co.uk

British Library Cataloguing in Publication Data
A catalogue record for this title is available from the British Library

ISBN 978 0 340 80425 4

First published 2001
Impression number   10 9 8 7
Year   2007

Hodder Headline's policy is to use papers that are natural, renewable and recyclable
products and made from wood grown in sustainable forests. The logging and
manufacturing processes are expected to conform to the environmental regulations of
the country of origin.

Digital artwork by David Hancock
Cartoons by Pat Murray
Cover design by Mike Stones
Typeset by J&L Composition Ltd, Filey, North Yorkshire
Printed in Great Britain for Hodder Arnold, an imprint of Hodder Education and a
member of the Hodder Headline Group, an Hachette Livre UK company,
338 Euston Road, London NW1 3BH by Martins the Printers Ltd, Berwick upon Tweed.

Contents

> All past questions are taken from Edexcel's Information Studies
> 1502 papers, a different but related specification

INTRODUCTION

WHAT IS BUSINESS AND COMMUNICATION SYSTEMS?

All people involved in business need access to all kinds of information and data in order to be able to do their jobs effectively. They receive this information through the various systems in place within each particular business. Business and Communication Systems, then, looks at:

- the systems of communication that are used within business and that support business

- how information and data is processed through these systems to ensure this information and data is reliable and makes sense

- how people know what is going on so they know what is expected of them and what to do.

What is a system?

A system is a set of connected parts that form a whole or that work together, for example, the railway system is a system of different railway companies that work together to form the UK's rail network.

Systems in business can be both manual and computer-based and it is the effectiveness of the systems that can influence how successfully the business is run. Those businesses that have the best information will always have an advantage over competitors.

When judging the effectiveness of systems, managers need to look at how good their control and improvement of communication, information/data and administration is and how good their systems are for receiving, processing, storing and communicating information.

When designing new systems or changing existing systems, managers might ask themselves the following questions.

How easy is the system to use?

Do employees need a lot of training to be able to operate the system because the system is complicated or is the operation pretty straightforward? If a lot of training is needed, then this will have a cost implication, as well as requiring employees to have to spend time actually acquiring the training. If the system does not make life easier or improve performance, then it is not working.

Does the system cause stress?

If employees have to undergo training, how do they view this? Some employees will welcome it and see it as a positive thing that will improve their skills, their career prospects, their chances of promotion and make their jobs easier.

Some employees will have the opposite view and be totally opposed to changes in the system(s). This can have the effect of making them feel stressed, anxious and unhappy, leading to low morale and less work being done.

How efficient is the system?

Does the system do what is required of it? If operation of a system does not lead to improved communication and does not make previously difficult jobs easier, then it is not effective. Some factors that can affect efficiency are:

- the difficulty experienced when trying to contact other parts of the business because lines of communication between management and staff and between the business and other organisations are closed or inaccessible
- the fact that there is a great deal of paperwork, which clogs the system up
- the system is bureaucratic, which means that there are too many rules and regulations that slow the system down
- the information or data needed cannot be accessed
- the information or data is not easy to understand and is not well organised.

So what can managers do to ensure systems are efficient? They can make changes to systems and the way the business communicates, but in order to do this they need to consider:

- the purpose of the system
- who will use the system
- the type of access needed
- legislation related to both employees using the system and to information held in the system.

The purpose of the system – the system may be for the processing of financial information, which will enable the managers to ascertain how successful the business is in terms of profit. Another purpose would be to co-ordinate and control communication within the business between different levels in the hierarchy. Yet another purpose might be the order processing system, which enables the business to sell and receive payment for its products or services.

Use of the system – the different users can include employees, shareholders and others outside the business, so the system has to be one they understand whatever their reason for use, whatever their expertise and wherever they are.

Access to the system – is access going to be restricted to certain users so information of a confidential nature is not available to everyone? This then poses the question of how security and confidentiality of information and data will be maintained and when will users need access – every day, weekly or real time, for example?

Legislation – what does the business have to do to comply with the terms of the various acts related to health and safety of employees and the protection of data and files?

Will the system mean employees are at more risk from eye strain, backache or repetitive strain injury? Will a security policy need to be considered to safeguard any personal data held in the system?

When managers have answered all the above questions they will be in a position to know what system or systems are best suited to them and their business. Do they go for the cheapest system or do they adopt the system that actually does what they want it to do regardless of cost? However, and this is very important, any system should be:

- secure
- reliable and
- not break the law.

COMMUNICATION SYSTEMS

PROCESS OF COMMUNICATION

At the end of this unit you should understand:

▸ what communication is

▸ the purpose of communication

▸ the process of communication

▸ different types of communication

▸ the benefits of good communication

▸ reasons for poor communication

▸ the effects of poor communication.

Look at these images.

What can you see?

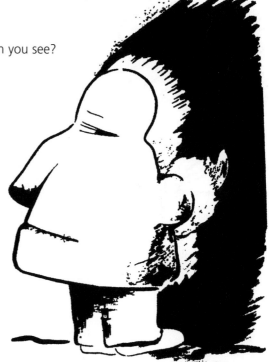

There are two images here, can you see them?

There are also two images here, can you see them?

What can you see here?

Some of us can see the images immediately, some of us cannot. We sometimes cannot even agree on what it is we are looking at. If this is so, it is not surprising that we sometimes get a communications breakdown. For example, during World War One, a platoon of soldiers sent a message to headquarters: 'Send reinforcements, we're going to advance.' Unfortunately, communication was not very good and the message received was: 'Send three and fourpence, we're going to a dance!' Not very funny for the soldiers waiting for the reinforcements.

(Try this exercise with the help of your teacher.)

Task 1.2

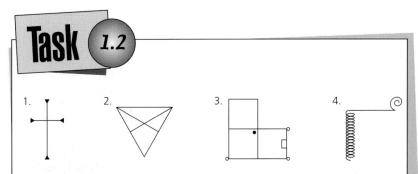

As a whole class, select a volunteer. The volunteer must describe the above shapes to the rest of the class. The rest of you must draw the shapes as described.

1 The volunteer stands with his/her back to the class. No questions can be asked.

2 The volunteer faces the class. No questions can be asked.

3 The volunteer faces the class. Questions can be asked.

4 The volunteer can demonstrate. Questions can be asked.

How difficult was it to communicate the shapes?

WHAT IS COMMUNICATION?

Communication is the passing of information between people.

All organisations need to be able to communicate with people in the organisation and with other organisations in this country and throughout the world. The most successful companies are those that encourage two-way communication – from senior personnel to employees and the other way around, from employees to senior personnel.

Organisations have to overcome problems of understanding. Not every message sent is meaningful to those who receive it. Poor wording and layout can create a bad impression. Any method of communication should be clear so all can understand the message or information being sent.

In international communication there is the language problem. Translators will be needed to translate if organisations deal with non-English-speaking countries.

The larger the organisation, the more difficult it is to ensure efficient communication. Methods and systems of communication have to be used that will keep everyone in touch and everyone informed.

There are many ways of communicating. These can include writing letters, speaking to people, face to face, using the telephone, sending e-mails and sending a fax, although there are many other ways of communicating.

Task 1.1

Try this exercise.

1 Read all the instructions carefully.

2 Get a clean sheet of A4 paper.

3 Put your name at the right-hand side of the paper.

4 Put the date at the left.

5 Number the paper in the bottom right-hand corner with the number 1.

6 Rule a right-hand 2 cm margin.

7 Number all the lines.

8 At the top, in the middle, draw a box 6 cm x 2 cm.

9 Write in the box 'I must read all instructions carefully'.

10 Only do No 1 above.

How did you do – did you follow instruction 1 only or did you get down to number 10?

Task 1.3

An urgent message has been received, which needs to be passed on to a member of staff in another part of the building.

a) How many ways can you think of for getting the message to the member of staff?

b) Which one do you think is the most appropriate and why?

c) What could happen if the message is not passed on or is not correct?

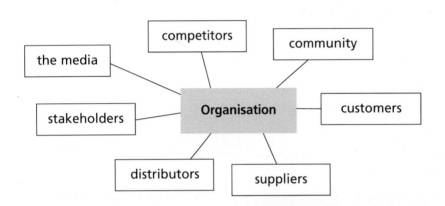

Good communication is essential for the efficient running of any business or organisation. Every organisation needs to communicate with a large number of people.

Task 1.4

What do you think each of the groups in the previous diagram would want to contact the organisation about? Using appropriate software, draw up a chart showing at least one reason why each group would want to contact the organisation.

For example:

THE MEDIA   to discuss rumours about a new product

The purpose of communication

The purpose of communication is:

■ to give information – to inform employees of a future meeting or to notify a manager of problems with software or to provide customers with details of an order

■ to collect information – such as personal details of employees which will be needed for personnel records, or market research data on sales of products

- to clear up problems – misunderstandings in the organisation must be sorted out in order to reassure employees over any grievance they may have or to keep customers happy with the service they receive

- to keep the organisation running smoothly – everyone knows what they are supposed to be doing and they do it to the best of their ability

- to give the organisation a positive public image by eliminating errors, managing problems and dealing efficiently with customers.

The process of communication

The process involves:

- the sender – the person intending to send the message whose responsibility it is to make sure that what they want to say is clear and straightforward

- the message itself

- the medium – how the message is to be sent, eg telephone, letter

- the receiver – the person who is being sent the message whose responsibility it is to listen or read carefully so there are no misunderstandings

- feedback – occurs when the message is confirmed and acted upon if necessary, the feedback will usually come from the receiver to the sender.

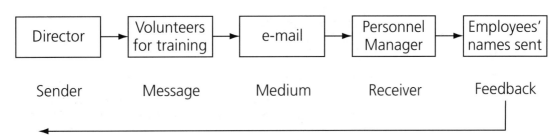

Process of communication

Internal communications

Internal communication takes place within an organisation, for example, between a manager and a supervisor or between two employees. It can take place in various directions:

- upwards

- downwards

- horizontal.

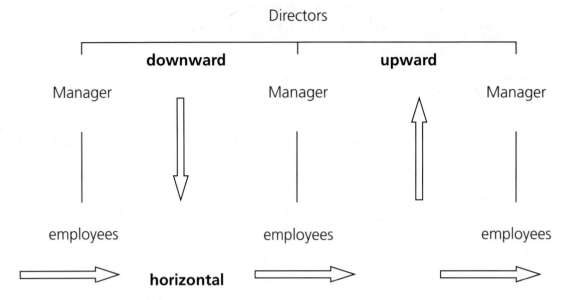

Direction of communication

Downward communication is usually used to tell employees about decisions made, instructions and company policy. It allows decisions to be put into practice and ensures all actions are co-ordinated and well-planned.

Upward communication is between employees and managers or directors. It can provide useful information about products and systems. It helps keep managers in touch with employees. It can also alert managers to potential problems.

Horizontal communication occurs between employees at the same level in the organisation. It can be between managers or between employees. In small organisations it occurs frequently and will tend to be informal because there are fewer employees.

Downward, upward and horizontal communication can also be said to be **formal communication**. This means official or approved communication channels within the organisation, for example departmental meetings.

There is also the **grapevine**. This is an unofficial or **informal** way of communicating and can be between people sharing a car, those who sit together for coffee or friends who work in different departments, for example. Communication through a grapevine can sometimes be a problem because messages and information get muddled. On the other hand, it can be a useful way of collecting information or passing on information.

External communications

External communications are those with people and groups outside the organisation, for example, customers, suppliers and the local community. The effectiveness with which these are carried out can affect the firm's image and reputation and help or hinder efficiency. It is important therefore that the organisation communicates well with these groups and keeps them informed at all times.

TYPES OF COMMUNICATION

There are five types of communication:

Written – letters, memoranda, reports, notices

Oral – telephone, face-to-face, meetings

Visual – charts, tables, posters, advertisements

Electronic – facsimile, computer, e-mail, pager

Non-verbal – body language.

It is the information that dictates which method is used depending upon:

- the nature of the information – is it long or short? Is it confidential?

- the speed with which it needs to be sent – does it need to be there today?

- whether it is best in written or oral form – would a telephone call be best?

- the cost – would the cost be too much?

Written communication

Written communication uses words, numbers and images. A record is kept of the message and it is possible to reach a large number of people at the same time.

Letters

A formal method of communication, which is usually external. It is possible to set out detailed instructions, confirm arrangements or pass on information. Letters can also be used internally for such matters as the appointment or dismissal of staff.

Advantages

- Letters can provide a permanent record for future reference.

- Accurate, clear messages can be sent.

Disadvantages

- They are slower than other methods, for example, telephone, e-mail.

- They can be less personal.

- There is no immediate feedback.

- If a secretary deals with correspondence, then the letter may not even be seen by the receiver.

Memoranda

Memo

To: T Brown
From: S Pike
Date: 4/8/01
Subject:

Following our recent meeting, I agree that the following ...

Memoranda or memos are usually used internally. They are usually brief and, as many organisations use computers, they are sent through internal electronic mail systems (e-mail).

Advantages

- They can provide a permanent record for future reference.

- They are short and to the point.

- If sent as e-mails, they can be sent out of work time to await the receiver, for example, from organisations in other countries with time differences.

Disadvantages

- There is no immediate feedback.

- If many e-mails are received, there is the possibility that some are missed and the receiver can suffer from information overload.

Reports

Reports are usually the result of some investigation or research, which is presented to others in the organisation. They are formal and structured and can deal with such things as health and safety, future plans or installation of new computers. The language should be simple and concise. They usually lead to action and help people make decisions.

REPORT

From:
To:
Date:

Introduction
Voice recognition software allows you
to talk to your computer...

Advantages

■ Reports can be copied and circulated to many people.

■ Reports usually deal with complicated matters, which are best dealt with in writing rather than by other methods.

Disadvantages

■ They can be complicated.

■ The language can be too difficult for some people to understand.

Notices

Notices are frequently used internally to communicate to employees within the organisation. They can be used to inform employees of forthcoming social events, job vacancies or fire drill procedures.

Advantages

■ They can be seen by a large number of people.

■ They are cheap to produce.

■ Notices are less time consuming than trying to contact each employee individually.

Disadvantages

■ Notices can be torn down or damaged.

■ There is no guarantee that everyone will read the notice.

Oral communication

Oral communication is communication via the spoken word. No record is usually kept.

Telephone

The telephone is a form of electronic communication, which provides fast communication within an organisation and with others outside the organisation. Mobile telephones ensure people can be contacted in case of urgency or emergency even when they are away from the organisation.

Advantages

- They provide two-way communication.
- Immediate feedback can be obtained.
- Problems can be sorted out quickly
- Information can be received quickly.

Disadvantages

- There is no written record of the conversation.
- Verbal messages can sometimes be misunderstood.
- The process can be time consuming if the person required is not available.
- When using mobile telephones, it is sometimes difficult to get a signal or the signal fails.

Face to face

Face-to-face communication is usually in the form of a **meeting**, which can be with one person or with many people.

Face-to-face communication can also be a one-to-one conversation or an informal chat.

Advantages

- Meetings ensure everyone gets the same message at the same time.
- Everyone can look at any paperwork and discuss any issues accordingly.
- Feedback can be given and received.
- The body language of the speaker can ensure the message is given effectively.
- Problems can be sorted out quickly.

Disadvantages

- In big meetings there is no way of telling whether everybody is listening.
- There is also no way of knowing whether everyone has understood the message.

- People are not always available for meetings.

- Not everyone is willing to speak up at meetings.

- Some people may have to travel, which is expensive in terms of time and cost.

Visual communication

An organisation can use charts, tables, pictures, maps, diagrams, photographs, films, videos and advertisements to attract people's attention. Visual communication gives impact to the information and usually simplifies it.

Charts and diagrams

These can be included in reports to show numerical data, which can be easier to understand than lots of complicated technical data. They enable trends to be seen at a glance.

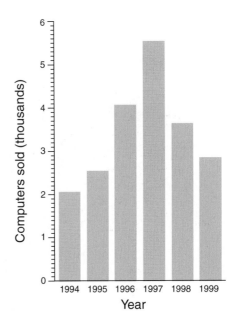

Tables

These are a simple way of presenting information. They present information clearly, whilst being simple to produce. If information is in prose form, it can be long-winded, but in a table it will be easier to understand.

Films and videos

These can be used to give information about the organisation, about the organisation's services or products or can be used in training of staff, for health and safety, for example.

Advertisements

These can be used to provide information about the organisation's services or products or persuade the customer to buy the company's product rather than that of a rival.

Advantages

- Information can be presented in a clearer way.

- The information can be seen as more interesting and appealing.

- Films and videos can show actual situations.

Disadvantages

- There is no feedback unless the organisation checks that the message has been received and understood.

Electronic communication

Facsimile (fax) machine

This is a way of sending black and white printed material or images between two organisations. The information is sent electronically between two fax machines using the telephone lines. The cost of sending the message depends upon the distance between the two organisations and the length of time it takes to transmit the message.

A fax has to contain certain information so that the receiver of the fax knows where it has come from and how many pages are being sent. The first page of the fax, therefore, is called the **fax header**.

Advantages

- Messages can be sent quickly when compared with letters.
- Exact copies of the message, image or drawing are sent.
- It is easy to send messages and no more complicated than a telephone call.

Disadvantages

- The received hard copy can sometimes be of poor quality.
- The sender and the receiver each need a fax machine.
- Can be time consuming feeding the sheets through.
- The fax machine can miss sheets.
- The message is not confidential.
- The fax machine can run out of paper in the middle of a fax transmission.

Electronic mail (e-mail)

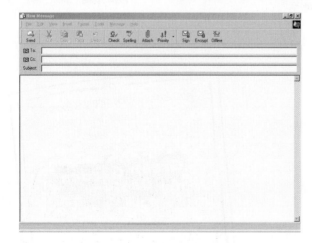

Electronic mail involves sending messages, data, files and graphics to other users on a computer network. Each person has an e-mail address, such as mlee@ems.hartlepool.sch.uk. Messages can be word-processed beforehand off-line and saved. Users then log-on and the message is sent quickly.

Advantages

- E-mail is useful to organisations spread over a number of different sites.
- Frequent contact can be made between users.

- Messages can be sent to a group of users.

- A printout can be made of messages.

- E-mail can be used at any time and messages left to await the receiver.

- Attachments can be made, which means other documents can be sent with the e-mail.

Disadvantages

- Users need a modem and a computer.

- Connections can sometimes be lost.

- It can sometimes be difficult to log on.

- Users have to subscribe to an ISP – Information Service Provider, for example AOL or Demon.

- Users have to check their mail boxes regularly.

- Users can forget to respond if not dealt with immediately.

- Some messages will need printing out, which can be time consuming and costly if the document is long.

Video conferencing

Video conferencing involves using computer links and closed circuit television, allowing people to hear and see each other.

Advantages

- Saves people travelling long distances for meetings.

- Savings are made in terms of time and cost.

- Face-to-face communication rather than telephone or letter.

Disadvantages

- The hardware required is still expensive.

- Needs a dedicated telephone line.

- People may prefer 'live' meetings.

- Everyone needs to be available.

- Connection or system could fail.

Pager

A pager is a device that is carried by the owner and enables him or her to be contacted in cases of urgency or an emergency or merely to pass on messages.

Advantages

- Very portable.

- Not expensive to buy.

- No extra rental charges.

Disadvantages

- No oral communication can take place.

- The pager has to be switched on.

- There is a charge for each message sent.

Non-verbal communication

Sometimes information is exchanged without speaking or writing. If no words are used, the communication is non-verbal, or body language is used. An expression or gesture, such as a frown, nod or smile, can indicate agreement or disagreement with a decision. Sometimes these non-verbal messages can be misinterpreted and people can receive the wrong message.

Task 1.5

For each of the following situations, suggest the most suitable communication method. Give your reasons.

1   Your Year Head wishes to inform all year 11 students of arrangements for the Christmas disco.

2   The head office of a software company wishes to inform its branches of changes in prices.

3   You need to send a copy of a job application form to a company immediately.

4   The managers of a company in Sunderland wish to discuss proposals with a company in Portsmouth.

5   There should be no smoking in the staff canteen.

6   The results of some market research into advantages of a new computer system.

7   Managers want to instruct all employees on how the new computer system works.

8   The Office Manager wants staff views on how waste paper could be reduced.

9   All workers need to know next year's holiday dates.

10 An applicant is invited for a job interview.

GOOD AND BAD COMMUNICATION

The benefits of good communication

Good communication is essential to any organisation because:

- it ensures that action is consistent and co-ordinated
- it ensures accurate and up-to-date information is given to employees and customers
- it encourages motivation in employees who will feel they have a say in the business
- a clear instruction ensures jobs get done well and on time
- it may help clear up misunderstandings
- it provides managers with information on which to base decisions
- it provides managers with feedback on previous decisions
- it is important to the image of the organisation.

Poor communication can lead to dissatisfied employees and customers, a poor business image and problems with others outside the organisation. Poor communication can mean employees do not understand what they have to do. If this happens, jobs can be duplicated and the motivation of the employees can be affected.

If customers are not satisfied this can lead to loss of orders and custom. Costs can be increased because work is not completed in the most efficient way, or mistakes are made and things are overlooked.

Reasons for poor communication

Sometimes communication is unsuccessful and messages are missed or misunderstood. This can lead to disputes and disagreements because important messages did not reach the person they were intended for. Problems may arise because:

- the language is too difficult for the receiver to understand because it is too technical or in another language
- the method chosen is unsuitable – a letter is sent when a telephone call would have been more appropriate
- the sender does not have the necessary skills to send the message – he or she cannot use e-mail and needs training
- feedback is not received, which would ensure the message was received and understood
- the receiver does not want to receive the message because he/she does not like the sender or wants to avoid the job

- the message is passed through too many people, which means the message gets confused and muddled
- there may be physical barriers, for example, a poor telephone line or background noise or poor visibility
- there is equipment breakdown, for example, no paper in fax machine or a low battery in a mobile phone.

Task 1.6

What communication problems are illustrated here?

'What's an ISDN line?'

'I should have had this information two days ago.'

'No confirmation was received about the meeting yesterday.'

'My mobile needs charging.'

'I can't use this program.'

'The train went through a tunnel so I lost the signal.'

The effects of poor communication

If good communication does not exist, things will not get done and problems will develop in the organisation.

- If managers do not keep in touch with employees' views and feelings then they will become discontented and unhappy. This could lead to frustration, a loss of motivation and could ultimately lead to industrial action.
- If customers are not happy with products and services they will become dissatisfied and could take their custom elsewhere, which could damage the firm's public image.
- Bad decisions based on incomplete, incorrect or misinterpreted information could result in lost business opportunities, which could lead to lost money and jobs.

Rules for good communication

If the following rules are followed, then communication will be efficient and less mistakes and confusion will occur.

Good communication should be:

- suitable for the intended audience – messages for different audiences require different methods of communication

- kept as simple as possible and unnecessary or irrelevant information should be avoided

- made as accurate and up-to-date as possible to avoid confusion, which can lead to mistakes being made.

Revision Questions

1 When someone is out of the building he or she can be contacted by a..............................

pager   swipe card   mouse   scanner

2 Some businesses use computers to talk to AND see their customers at the same time. This is known as ....

personal   video-   networking   interviews
contact   conferencing

3 If e-mail is used to communicate this means ....

computer-   using a   express   using a fax
to-computer   report   post

4 One manager sends a short message to another manager using a...........................

memorandum   report   letter   questionnaire

5 Managers hold regular meetings. This form of communication is..................................

e-mail   face to face   written   vertical

6 A business communicates with its suppliers by ....

memo   questionnaire   letter   notice

7 To display safety rules a business might use a ....

letter   report   notice   memo

8 An informal system of communication is a ....

grapevine   letter   report   notice

9 Information passed from a manager to an employee is ....

downward   horizontal   upward   diagonal

10 When someone is out of the office they can be contacted by a ....

pager   swipe card   mouse   scanner

Task 1.7

An important aspect of all businesses is good internal and external communication. Explain TWO consequences of having an inefficient communication system. (6 marks)

Task 1.8

You work for a firm that produces computer software. The firm has had a rush order and the production manager arranges an immediate meeting with the production supervisor.

1 Explain why the production manager has a meeting with the supervisor rather than using the telephone.

2 You have been asked to produce a memo informing all employees that, due to the rush order, they may be required to work overtime. Why is a memo for staff more appropriate than a notice? (4 marks)

(Adapted from Edexcel, 1999 – F and H)

Extension task

Good communication is often seen as vital to the efficient running of a firm. What factors might cause this communication to break down? Explain the implications of poor communication and suggest ways of improving these poor communication systems.

(12 marks)

COMMUNICATION SYSTEMS

PAPER-BASED SYSTEMS

At the end of this unit you should be able to:

▸ create and use newsletters, reports, letters, memoranda and notices

▸ complete forms

▸ create and use a notice of meeting, agenda, minutes, itineraries and schedules

▸ create and use flowcharts and diagrams of operating systems.

Paper-based forms of communication systems are used for situations where:

▪ speed is not particularly important

▪ long or complicated messages are to be sent

▪ the message is recorded for future reference or use

▪ it is necessary to contact several people at the same time

▪ people cannot be contacted by any other way.

NEWSLETTERS

Newsletters are paper-based informal printed reports, which give information that is of interest to, for example, employees in a business, members of a club or the parents of pupils in your school.

AJS Sports News

New Equipment
We are lucky to be receiving a government grant for new fitness equipment, which will be installed within the next couple of months. If there are any requests for certain types of equipment, please contact the club's vice-chairman, Mark.

The fitness area is now open on Mondays from 10am to 3pm. With a women only workout from 9am to 10 am

A brand new menu and selection of soft drinks are now available from our Juice Bar. The licensed bar is open from 7pm to 11pm

Task 2.1

Try and get hold of some examples of newsletters and compare the different types of information contained in them and the different layouts.

Newsletters are easy to produce using a word-processor and/or desk top publishing (DTP). Both word-processors and DTP programs can be used to create the text for the newsletters. Whether the text is imported into the DTP program or whether the word-processor only is used, both can combine text and graphics to give you the layout you want.

Facilities and special effects can be used to enhance the appearance of the newsletter:

■ borders, lines, columns, shapes (eg circles, rectangles or squares)

■ graphics (eg pictures, illustrations, clip art and images)

■ fonts and font sizes

■ positioning and resizing of graphics and text

■ colour.

White space is the space seen after pictures, clip art and images are placed on the page. In order to make best use of the space available, care should be taken with the use of this space.

Task 2.2

1 Using suitable software and some of the examples you have collected as a guide, design a newsletter on a topic of your own choice. Remember to include some of the facilities mentioned above.

2 When everyone in the class has completed their newsletters, compare them by making notes on:

■ suitability for intended audience

■ quality of design

■ accuracy

■ use of facilities, eg fonts, display, use of white space.

3 Combine the results of the whole class then identify which three newsletters come out best.

REPORTS

Reports are generally internal documents. They can be simple and short. They can be complex, with several headings, sub-headings and numbered paragraphs, and run into many pages. Headings or numbers are used to divide up different pieces of information. If these were not used, the report would simply be paragraph after paragraph of information and it would be very difficult to find specific points. However long they are, they must show information as clearly as possible.

Reports are written for different purposes and different audiences, for example:

- an accountant's report on the financial state of a company
- a health and safety officer's report on the fire precautions in a school
- a teacher's report on a pupil
- a head of year's report on a pupil's behaviour
- a personnel officer's report on an incident in the workplace
- a police officer's report on a burglary.

Reports are formal documents and tend to be impersonal. The reader should be considered when writing a report and the language therefore should not be too complicated or difficult to understand.

The layout of the report (see next page)

The layout will vary between organisations but all reports should contain:

- title
- terms of reference/introduction
- collection of data or research/procedure
- findings
- conclusions
- recommendations.

LETTERS

Letters sent from one organisation to another are called business letters. They are the most commonly used form of external written communication. A letter that is clearly and concisely written, correctly spelt and well displayed, will convey to the recipient a better impression of the writer and the firm than an untidy letter containing grammatical errors and spelling mistakes.

REPORT

FROM

DATE

SUBJECT   (*this will be the title of the report*)

1   **Terms of reference/introduction**

This is the introduction saying who asked for the report, why it is required (ie what it is about) and what the deadline is.

The report will advise the IT Manager on the implications of installing a new network system in order to provide efficient communications because of the opening of the new manufacturing site. The cost of the new system will be researched, as well as the implications for training of staff and the on-going maintenance of the system. The deadline is 200–.

2   **Collection of data or research/procedure**

This sets out how the information is to be gathered and what research methods will be used. You will be collecting information from a number of sources and you will need to say what these sources are – interviews with people, books, manuals, brochures etc.

3   **Findings**

This gives the information that has been requested. You will need to decide how to present this information so that it is easy to follow and understand. You may use spreadsheet, database or desktop publishing software to create tables, graphs and charts to show your findings. You will need to use sub-headings or numbered paragraphs, for example 3.1 or 3.1.1 or 3.1i or 3.1a.

4   **Conclusions**

Here you give a summary of the main findings. It is useful for people who do not wish to read the detailed findings.

5   **Recommendations**

These are your suggestions based on your findings. If you have not been asked to make any recommendations, you can omit this section.

An example of the layout for a short report

The requirements of a good letter are:

- the information, grammar and spelling should be correct
- the wording should be polite and easy to understand
- the letter should be displayed properly
- each new subject or point requires a new paragraph.

The advantages of letters are:

- they provide a permanent record for future reference

- the recipient of the letter has time to consider the contents of the letter before replying

- they can be cheaper than other methods, such as telephoning, particularly when telephoning abroad

- enclosures can be sent with the letter

- the contents cannot usually be misinterpreted.

The disadvantages are:

- they can be slow when compared with other methods, eg telephone, e-mail

- the sender has to wait for feedback

- they can take up a lot of storage space

- delivery can sometimes be unreliable.

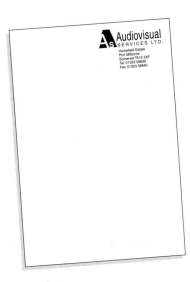

The official notepaper of a business is called the **letterhead**. The letterhead will contain the company's name, address, telephone and fax numbers and e-mail address. It might also include other information like the names of directors, VAT number, the company logo and the company's website address.

The most common form of layout for business letters is **fully blocked** and **open punctuation**. This means that all lines are blocked to the left-hand margin and punctuation is only used in the actual message part or body of the letter.

Formal business letters should follow these rules:

1 If a **reference** is included, it is usually the initials of the writer of the letter and the person preparing the letter eg SG/FT/23593.

2 The **date** the letter is written is included. It is usually written as 28 September 20--.

3 The name and address of the person to whom the letter is being sent is called the inside address or **addressee**.

4 The **salutation** is the words of greeting that begin the letter.

5 The **heading** lets the reader know what the letter is about.

Fully blocked letter with open punctuation on company letterhead

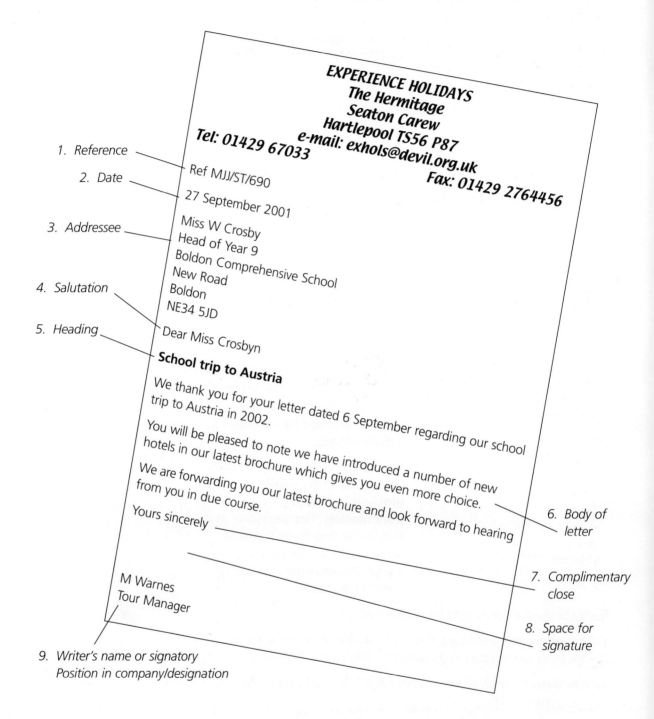

1. Reference

2. Date

3. Addressee

4. Salutation

5. Heading

EXPERIENCE HOLIDAYS
The Hermitage
Seaton Carew
Hartlepool TS56 P87
Tel: 01429 67033
e-mail: exhols@devil.org.uk
Fax: 01429 2764456

Ref MJJ/ST/690

27 September 2001

Miss W Crosby
Head of Year 9
Boldon Comprehensive School
New Road
Boldon
NE34 5JD

Dear Miss Crosbyn

School trip to Austria

We thank you for your letter dated 6 September regarding our school trip to Austria in 2002.

You will be pleased to note we have introduced a number of new hotels in our latest brochure which gives you even more choice.

We are forwarding you our latest brochure and look forward to hearing from you in due course.

Yours sincerely

M Warnes
Tour Manager

6. Body of letter

7. Complimentary close

8. Space for signature

9. Writer's name or signatory
Position in company/designation

6   The **body of the letter** contains the message. If the letter is to be brief, you may find the 'three paragraph' rule helpful. The first paragraph is an introduction, the second paragraph contains the message and the third paragraph suggests future action.

7   Make sure you end with the correct **complimentary close** – Yours faithfully or Yours sincerely.

When the letter begins with Dear Sir or Dear Madam it should end with Yours faithfully – notice the capital Y of Yours and the small f of faithfully.

When the letter begins with a name – Dear Mrs Watson – then it should end with Yours sincerely – again notice the capital Y of Yours and the small s of sincerely.

8   Five or six line spaces should be left under the company name for the **signature** of the person writing the letter.

9   The name of the person sending the letter (the **signatory**) should be printed underneath the space left for the signature because some signatures can be difficult to read. Their position in the company is usually also included. This is called the **designation**.

Task 2.3

W R Smith Insurance Co of 96 York Road, Hartlepool TS22 7PU are sending the following letter. Use suitable software to prepare the following letter. Remember to spellcheck and proofread before printing out.

Insert a suitable reference

Insert the date

Miss A Dodds
21 Elmwood Street
Throston
Hartlepool
TS23 S45

Dear Miss Dodds

Vacancy – Office Junior

Thank you for your letter of application regarding the above vacancy.

Mrs Philips will be pleased to interview you on Monday (*insert an appropriate date*) at 10.30 am.

Please bring your Record of Achievement with you.

Yours sincerely

Miss J Welsh
Office Manager

Task 2.4

Use suitable software to prepare the following letter. Remember to spellcheck and proofread before printing out.

Ref   Date it today

Miss T. Henderson, Pike Electronics, 16–18 York Rd, Hartlepool TS25 7OR. Dear Miss Henderson, Thank you for your enquiry about a new printer.

As requested I have made arrangements for our representative to call on Monday (insert an appropriate date) at 10.30 am to give you a demonstration.

I hope this is convenient for you.

Yours sincerely Mark Winterton, Sales Manager

Task 2.5

Use suitable software to prepare the following letter. Use fully-blocked layout and open punctuation. Remember to spellcheck and proofread before printing out. You work for Pike Electronics.

Write a letter to Brown & Taylor Software, City House, Trafalgar Road, Middlesbrough, TS78 P99. Dear Sirs, Order No SS8890, With reference to the above order placed with you two months ago, it would be appreciated if you would now give us a firm delivery date. When we placed this order with you, delivery was promised within 14 days. We are now completely out of stock of this software package and we would be pleased if you would despatch this order immediately, otherwise we are afraid we must cancel the order. We await speedy delivery of this software. Yours faithfully, E Rogers, Manager.

MEMORANDA

A memorandum or memo is an internal message sent between employees of the same firm. Memos are intended to be informal between colleagues, which is why no salutation or complimentary close is necessary. The messages tend to be brief and to the point and they are not signed although some people like to initial them thinking that this gives the message a more personal touch. Like letters, a memo provides a written record of the messages sent.

Memos are sometimes written on pre-printed forms with spaces for:

■ the name of the sender

■ the name of the receiver

MEMORANDUM

TO: DATE:
FROM: REF:
SUBJECT:
_____

■ the date sent

■ sometimes space for a reference

■ sometimes space for a heading

■ a brief message.

Some companies have their own in-house style and the memo below is another example of layout.

MEMORANDUM

TO: Senior Clerk
FROM: IT Manager
DATE: 21 March 20--
REF: FF/LO
_____

Received your memo this afternoon and would like to ask you to look into a few details.

a) How many boxes of printer paper will you require for the next 3 weeks?

b) Will you require any more toner before the end of the month?

c) Have there been any problems with the new laser printers installed last week?

As many businesses use computer networks, electronic mail or e-mail has increasingly replaced the memo as a short, quick way of communicating. The computer creates its own pre-set format and the sender fills in the spaces.

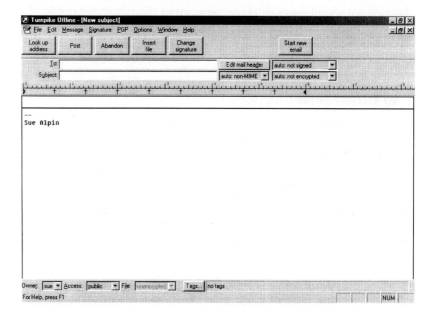

Task 2.6

Docdel plc is starting a new training programme for employees from 1 June 20--. Prepare a memo from Head Office to all Showroom Managers informing them of the new training programme that starts in June. (4 marks)

(Edexcel, 1997 – F)

Task 2.7

Laura Hughes has asked you to prepare a memo to all employees informing them that, due to the rush order for ginger ice cream, they may be required to work overtime. Prepare an appropriate memo. (4 marks)

(Edexcel, 1999 – F and H)

NOTICES

A notice is a printed announcement. It can be internal or external.

An internal notice could be used, for example, to announce a social event in the business or it could be a safety notice.

An external notice could be used, for example, to inform the public of the closure of the business for a short time due to renovation or to advertise a forthcoming concert.

The advantages of notices are:

■ they can be seen by many people

■ they are a relatively cheap way of informing people

■ if done well, notices can attract people's attention.

The disadvantages are:

■ they can be torn and quickly start to look messy and unattractive

■ not everyone may see the notice.

There are no strict rules for producing notices and, as with newsletters, you can use whatever facilities you have available. Display is important because the whole point of a notice is to catch people's attention. You have to try and make notices attractive and eye-catching. Be careful, however, not to make the notice too cluttered because this can make it difficult to read. In addition, if you use too many facilities you can make the notice look untidy.

The notice below has been centred across and down the page. Bold, underscore and italics have also been used.

PUBLIC NOTICE

Christmas and New Year Holidays

These offices will be closed from December 21 2001
until January 2002

It depends upon the content of the notice as to what layout you use – sometimes blocked style is more appropriate particularly for something like a price list because it makes it easier to read.

BROWNS HOTEL

The following are the daily terms at Browns until the end of the year

Bed and Breakfast

Bed and Breakfast with Evening Meal

Full Board

£25.00

£40.00

£55.00

Some notices are so important that they must be seen by everybody.

FIRE ACTION

IF YOU HEAR THE FIRE ALARM

Leave by the nearest Exit
DO NOT stop to collect personal belongings
Close all doors as you leave
DO NOT re-enter the building
Assemble at the rear of the building
Ensure that the Fire Brigade has been called

Task 2.8

Use suitable software and produce a notice for your Christmas Disco. Remember to include the date, venue, time, price, whether refreshments are available and any other information you think appropriate.

Task 2.9

1 The Production Manager has asked you to design a notice to be displayed in the production area. His rough notes are shown below. His spelling is poor so you will need to correct any errors you find. (10 marks)

HEADING: CRISIS MANAGEMENT
THE FOLLOWING RULES APPLY IF ANY GLASS IS BROKEN IN THE PRODUCTION AREA

② ALL ICE-CREAM IN THE PRODUCTION AREA TO BE DESTROYED

③ ALL EQUIPMENT TO BEE STRIPPED AND CLEANED

④ INVESTIGATION BY PRODUCTION MANGER INTO CAUSE

⑤ PRODUCTION ONLY TO BE RESTARTED ON AUTHORITY OF PRODUCTION MANAGER

① ALL PRODUCTION TO BE STOPED

⑥ PRODUCTION MANAGER TO REPORT TO COMPLETE INCIDENT REPORT TO MANAGING DIRECTOR

2 Why do you think it is important to have such a notice displayed in a production area? (3 marks)

(Edexcel – 1999 F)

FORMS

Much of the communication that takes place within organisations is by means of forms. The issuer of the form is able to ask precisely what is required and there is usually no opportunity for the person completing the form to waffle or give irrelevant information.

We are required to fill in a great many pre-printed forms. For example:

- year 9 option form
- job application
- passport application
- bank account application
- sixth form entry application
- student loan or grant forms
- university application (UCAS form)
- telephone message forms.

Forms need to be filled in by hand and it is very important that they are clear and correct. Although this should make for clear and efficient communication, some people still fill in forms poorly. For example, how many of you, when filling in a form, have put your telephone number in the space for date of birth or put your registration group where your age should be?

This inevitably leads to delay, misunderstanding and additional expense – in time and money. Like any other form of communication breakdown, it can also lead to frustration and irritation.

When you fill in a form, for any reason, remember the following rules:

1 Read the instructions carefully – are you asked to use block capitals, a black pen etc?

2 Read the questions carefully – do not cram an answer into a tiny space or put the wrong answer in.

3 Give all dates and times accurately.

4 Delete inappropriate details when asked to, eg Mr, Mrs, Miss or Ms.

5 Never leave blanks – someone may think you have overlooked this question – write 'not applicable' or 'N/A'.

6 Do not forget to sign the form.

7 Always write neatly.

Sometimes an application form is your first contact with an organisation and you want to make a good impression. If you can, photocopy the form and use this as a draft. If this is not possible try filling it in in pencil and then going over in ink to ensure you do not make any mistakes. If you do make a mistake and you are tempted to use correcting fluid be careful because this can be messy. It might be better to cross the mistake out neatly and add the correction.

Task 2.10

A large hotel is opening in your town. Your local newspaper carries the following advertisement for a number of jobs in the hotel.

Opening January

THE FRIENDLY INN

A new 3-star hotel on the outskirts of town

STAFF REQUIRED

TRAINEE CHEF
Good opportunities within this well-known hotel chain to train under chef of high renown.
Ref 9878

WAITERS/WAITRESSES
Tidy appearance. Pleasant manner. Silver Service training given.
Ref 9879

RECEPTIONISTS
Neat and pleasant appearance. Good telephone manner essential. Friendly personality. Training given. Opportunities to attend college on day release.
Ref 9880

CHAMBERMAIDS
Conscientious and dependable. No formal qualifications or prior experience needed as training will be given.
Ref 9881

Contact Mrs V Beresford at The Job Centre for an application form

---

1 Study the advert and select the job that most appeals to you.

2 Complete the application form your teacher will give you (see the Teacher's book), giving details of your interests on the back of the form.

3 Why do you think it is important to take care with the presentation of this application form?

BUSINESS MEETINGS

Any large business will organise meetings to communicate and discuss issues that are important to the business. These could be departmental meetings, meetings of the managers or meetings of employees. In school, you might go to meetings of the School Council. Each of these meetings will have different matters to discuss but because these are formal meetings there are a few basic rules that should be followed.

Those people required to attend a meeting must be informed of the date, time and place. This is usually done by means of a **notice of meeting**. The period of notice to be given could be between seven and 21 days.

WOODRUSH HIGH SCHOOL

Notice of Meeting

of Academic Board to be held in room B34 on Wednesday 24 October 2001 at 15.45.

A G E N D A

1 Apologies for absence (*received from those unable to be at the meeting*)

2 Minutes of the last meeting (*the minutes or notes made from the last meeting are read*)

3 Matters arising from the minutes (*discussion and follow-up of matters or decisions taken at the last meeting*)

4 Curriculum (*discussion on this topic*)

5 Sixth form (*discussion on this topic*)

6 Any other business (*AOB – at this point members bring up points or questions not included in the agenda*)

7 Date and time of next meeting (*agreed before members leave the meeting*)

The **agenda** is a list of what is to be discussed at the meeting. It is circulated to members before the meeting in order to give them time to study the items for discussion.

The agenda items are arranged in order of discussion. Items 1, 2 and 3 always appear on the agenda. Items for discussion are next, then there is usually an item at the end called **any other business**. This allows discussion of matters of interest that are not already on the agenda. The final item, **date of next meeting**, is useful so that members can agree a mutually convenient date for the next meeting before they depart.

One member at the meeting will take the **minutes**, which are a record of what takes place in the meeting and of any decisions that have been reached. These provide a clear and accurate record of what was discussed. It is important that they are:

- accurate because they should provide a true account of the meeting

- reasonably brief because their aim is to present a summary only of the main points of discussion

- clear because they provide the only record of discussion and decisions for those members who were unable to be present at the meeting.

Minutes of Academic Board of Woodrush High School held in B34 on Wednesday 24 October 2001 at 15.45.

Present:

Mr G Linden	Dr M Lister	Mr D Woods
Mrs C Watts	Mr K Philips	Mr N Quinn
Ms T Sorenson	Miss S Varga	Mr M Gray

1 Apologies for absence: Miss L Price, Mr T Leslie.

2 Minutes of last meeting
The minutes of the meeting held on Wednesday 26 September 2001 were approved.

3 Matters arising
The point raised by Mr Quinn at the previous meeting with regard to the new design for school reports has been discussed by the Pastoral Board and agreed by them. These will now go to the printer.

4 Curriculum
Mr Linden reported on the programme of discussions with Heads of Department. The analysis of exam results in 20-- is now almost complete. He distributed the analysis from HBC, which shows positive value added.

5 Sixth form issues
Miss Varga reported on sixth form issues. Some students are planning to drop from 4 to 3 AS subjects. Miss Varga is contacting parents.

There appears to be increased pressure on the time students have and this was causing concern with tutors. Concern was also expressed about the problem of accommodation with our increased numbers. Mr Linden said SMT were looking at this with a view to leasing mobiles.

It was agreed to discuss the problem of accommodation at the next meeting.

6 Any other business
Mr Linden reminded Heads of Department about the year 6 Open Evening on November 1.

Mrs Watts reminded Heads of Department of the joint Art Textiles and Technology project underway.

7 Date of next meeting
9 December 20--.

Task 2.11

You are required to prepare a Notice, Agenda and Minutes for a meeting.

In groups, decide the subject of your meeting – it could be the committee responsible for the year 10 Christmas Disco or the year 11 Leavers Dinner – it's up to you to decide.

In discussion with the rest of the group, decide when and where the meeting will be held, together with the topics to be discussed.

If you can, actually hold the meeting and prepare the minutes.

Do not worry that the notices, agendas and minutes will be very similar with regard to content – they are bound to be when they are all on the same topic.

Task 2.12

1 What is the notice of a meeting?

2 What is the agenda?

3 Explain THREE advantages of holding a meeting.

4 Why is it important to have an accurate account of a meeting?

(12 marks)

ITINERARIES

An itinerary is a route of a journey or a list of places to be visited on a journey. It can contain:

- the departure and arrival times of aeroplanes and trains
- flight numbers or train times
- airport names, terminal names/numbers or station names
- useful addresses, telephone numbers and names of contacts
- hotel addresses and telephone numbers.

The 24 hour clock is used to save confusion that can arise between am and pm. Itineraries tend to be produced on paper or card of a size that can be handled easily, ie kept in a purse or wallet for easy reference.

ITINERARY

Wednesday 14 February 20--

Depart Hartlepool for bus journey to Heathrow – Terminal 4	0600
Depart Heathrow for New York (JFK Airport) Flight No BA445	1710
Arrive JFK Airport	2020

Sunday 17 February 2001

Depart Quality Hotel, Broadway, New York for JFK Airport	1500
Depart JFK Airport, Flight No BA446	2000
Arrive Heathrow Terminal 4 approximately	0900
Arrive Hartlepool approximately	1600

Task 2.13

Get a copy of a train/bus timetable or holiday brochure and plan an itinerary for a journey you wish to make.

SCHEDULES

A schedule can be a list, catalogue, a timetable or programme. Probably the schedule you are most familiar with would be a schedule of events, leading to something like year nine option choices, as shown below.

SCHEDULE OF YEAR NINE ACTIVITIES DURING OPTIONS WEEK	
Monday	Art Day – activities presented by the Art Department, including ceramics, textiles, printmaking and photography
Tuesday	Technology Day – activities presented by various local companies, eg Orchid Drinks, Stadium Electronics and Sweet and Savoury
Wednesday	Business Day – activities organised and run by students from Sunderland University based on a business theme
Thursday	Parents are given the opportunity of meeting all subject teachers at 6.30 pm in St Annes Hall
Friday	Option Talks by all subject option teachers in a special assembly in St Annes Hall

Your completed Options Forms must be handed to Mr Lee during PSE next Friday.

As you can see, the schedule is a timetable or programme of planned events. This can be circulated to all interested parties to ensure they all know what is happening when and where.

FLOWCHARTS

A flowchart shows the step-by-step progression through a process from beginning to end.

The flow chart opposite shows how a mail order catalogue works from the customer's point of view. As you can see, the points are one below the other, joined by downward arrows.

A more complicated flowchart can show the flow of information or documents in both directions.

The flowchart below shows the flow of documents between a buyer and seller in a business transaction.

Customer selects goods from catalogue
↓
Customer orders goods
↓
Catalogue company delivers goods to customer
↓
Company sends invoice to customer
↓
Customer pays the invoice

A basic flowchart

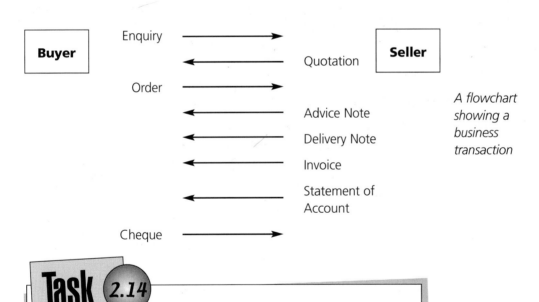

A flowchart showing a business transaction

Task 2.14

Draw a simple flowchart of milk getting from the cow to your doorstep in time for your breakfast each day.

OPERATING SYSTEMS

The most important piece of system software in a computer system is the **operating system** that controls it. It is a program or a set of programs that manages the operation of the computer and is usually represented on paper like the example below. The use of arrows in both flow charts and operating systems guides the reader through the sequence of operations or tasks.

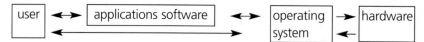

The operating system has to be loaded into the main memory once the computer has been switched on before any other programs can be run. The operating system deals with instructions from the user to save, load, delete, rename and copy files.

It also controls the use of peripherals such as disk drives and printers and it displays messages about errors and problems such as a printer running out of paper.

Revision Questions

1 To display safety rules in the workshops, Louisa Designs might use a ....

  letter   report   notice   minutes

2 If Louisa signed a letter 'Yours faithfully', it would begin ....

  Dear Sir   Dear John   Dear Mr Roberts   Dear John Roberts

3 What is a list of places to be visited on a journey?

  application form   itinerary   questionnaire   schedule

4 What is a list of things to be discussed at a meeting?

  memo   notice   flow chart   agenda

5 The directors of Harbon Estates Ltd use a .... to send a short message to a departmental manager?

  memorandum   report   letter   questionnaire

6 Nocha Ltd's letters to clients have no punctuation in the body of the letter. This is known as ....

  fully blocked   indented paragraphs   open punctuation   left justified

7 Collectors wanting to join the Happy Ideas Ltd Club must first complete ....

  an application form   a memorandum   a telephone message   a facsimile

8 How many spaces should be left for the signature of a letter? ....

  five   seven   ten   twelve

9 The position in the company of a person sending a letter is known as the ....

  signatory   designation   addressee   reference

10 To ensure you have not overlooked a question on a form you would insert ....

  your date of birth   your surname   N/A   your postcode

Extension task

The directors of Delta Homes plc intend to improve the way their company communicates.

The current methods of communication include:

WRITTEN	VERBAL
Memoranda	Meetings
Letters	Teams
Reports	Interviews
Notices	Presentations
Minutes	

Suggest the items of communications hardware and software that the directors of Delta Homes plc should purchase. Evaluate the improvements in communication that these will bring.

(20 marks)

(Edexcel, 1998 – H)

three

COMMUNICATION SYSTEMS

ORGANISATIONS

INTERNAL SYSTEMS

When a business has a number of employees some form of **organisational structure** is necessary. These organisational structures take into account the following:

■ who is in charge

■ who has the authority to make decisions

■ who carries out decisions

■ how information is communicated in the business.

This is so that the employees, or anyone outside the business, know who makes the decisions and who does what in the business.

Imagine the chaos if no one knew who worked where, who did what and how to communicate with particular individuals.

Organisation charts

Many businesses produce **organisation charts** like the one overleaf, which sets out the organisation structure.

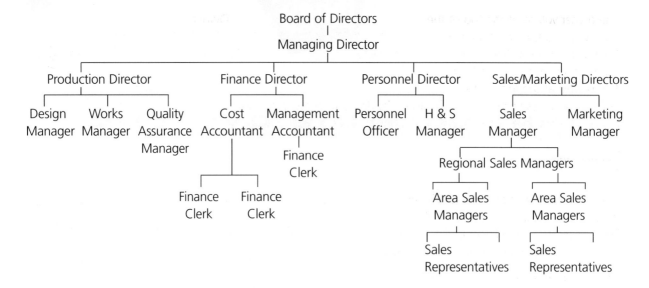

Different businesses will have different organisation charts but the style for all organisation charts will be similar.

So why do businesses have organisation charts?

They have organisation charts so that:

- if information is not being received the breakdown can be highlighted by tracing it through the chart

- employees can see where they are in the organisation, who has authority over them and who they take orders from

- it can be seen how each part of the business relates to other parts.

Draw an organisation chart for your school or college. You may find this is complicated because some people will have more than one responsibility in the school – some teachers may teach their subject as well as act as a form tutor. Good luck!

Hierarchy

A small business which employs few employees probably has an organisation structure that is less formal than a larger business. This is because the employees probably see each other many times each day and communication takes place continually and easily.

The **hierarchy** is what we call the number of levels of responsibility or management in a business from the lowest to the highest. In a small business, there is likely to be at most two levels like the one in the hierarchy below.

The owner will be at the top of the hierarchy because he or she has the major responsibility in the business. Most businesses have few people at the top of the structure and many more at the bottom. This leads to a structure that looks like a pyramid – narrow at the top and wide at the bottom.

Chain of command

The hierarchy also shows the **chain of command**, which is the way in which orders pass down the levels and information passes up the levels.

The person at the top of the hierarchy is in overall control of the business and has the most authority.

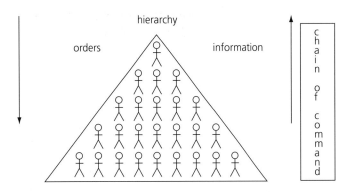

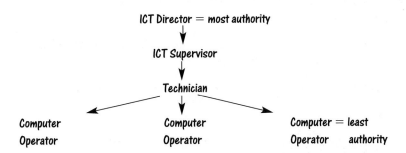

The above is a chain of command for a business involved with information communications technology. There are no rules about the number of links in the chain but businesses generally try to keep chains as short as possible because it is then easier for managers and employees to communicate.

It is thought that the longer the chain of command the more difficulties the business can face, for example:

- messages can be slowed down, lost or distorted because of the number of levels through which they must pass, like Chinese whispers

- managers at the top of the chain might be seen as being remote and not in touch with employees lower down the chain or hierarchy.

Span of control

The **span of control** is the number of people directly controlled by one person. The Technician in the chain of command above has a span of control of three. This is the number of people he or she has direct authority over. In this case, the Technician has authority over the three Computer Operators.

A narrow span of control means that the person has authority over only two or three people. A wide span of control means that the person has authority over a large number of people.

Having a narrow span of control means that managers have:

■ tighter control and closer supervision over employees

■ time to think and plan without having to worry about supervising many employees with minor day-to-day problems and issues

■ better communication with employees beneath them – subordinates – because of the small number of employees.

Tall organisation pyramid

However, a disadvantage is that this may lead to too many levels of management. This kind of **tall organisation**, as it is called, can be difficult to run.

A wider span of control means managers have responsibility for more employees. If managers have more people to manage, this means that:

■ they might **delegate** more

■ they must have far more trust in subordinate staff to get on with their jobs because they haven't much time to supervise

■ subordinates might have more opportunity for decision-making

■ subordinates may be more motivated because of the trust and responsibility they are given.

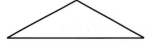

Flat organisation pyramid

Having a wider span means fewer managers are needed and this gives a hierarchy with fewer levels, which is called a **flat organisation**.

Delegation

If managers have more to do, they cannot do everything themselves so they **delegate** to subordinates. Delegation means giving a subordinate the authority to perform a particular task. You must remember though that it is the authority to perform a task that is being delegated, not the final responsibility. If the job is done badly by the subordinate, then it is the senior person who has to accept the responsibility for this.

Delegation has advantages for the manager as:

■ they cannot do everything themselves therefore it makes sense to delegate

■ they are less likely to make mistakes because they can concentrate on important things and not be distracted by minor problems

■ they can see how well their staff are performing when given added duties and responsibilities.

Advantages for the subordinate are:

■ their work becomes more interesting and rewarding, leading to increased job satisfaction

■ they feel more valued and enjoy the trust placed in them

■ delegation helps to train employees, which gives them more skills, which helps their career opportunities with perhaps promotion or progression in the business.

Smiths is a company that manufactures computer hardware. Their organisation structure is shown below. Using this chart answer the following questions.

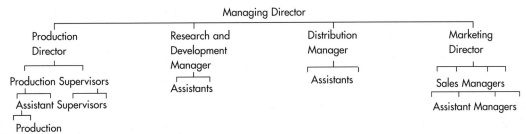

1   With reference to the chart explain the following terms:

   a) chain of command
   b) hierarchy.   (4 marks)

2   A number of possible problems have been identified with its organisational structure. These include:

   ■ the number of managers, assistant supervisors and assistant managers

   ■ the roles and responsibilities of all employees

   ■ communication and decision-making.

   Again, using the diagram, explain any possible problems the company might be experiencing.   (6 marks)

3   Explain how Smiths might solve these problems.   (4 marks)

Task 3.3

Rose Elliott opened her first secretarial agency 20 years ago. Over that time, the business has grown rapidly with the increasing demand for secretarial, clerical and word processing services, as well as the increasing need for providing temporary staff.

She now has five large agencies and ten smaller agencies in different towns. She is planning to open another agency but is worried because her job has changed so much. She says she seems to spend her time organising other managers and rarely has time to see her customers. Recruiting the right staff is vital to the success of her business.

Her organisational structure is shown below.

1   With reference to the chart above, explain the following terms:

   a) span of control
   b) delegation.   (4 marks)

2   a) What is an organisation chart?
   b) Explain TWO advantages to the business of having an organisation chart.   (6 marks)

3   Since the business has grown Rose has had to delegate some of her duties.

   a) Explain TWO advantages to Rose and the business of delegation.   (4 marks)
   b) Give TWO examples of decisions that you would expect Rose to delegate. Give reasons
      for your answers.
                                                                          (6 marks)

   c) Give TWO examples of decisions that you WOULD NOT advise Rose to delegate.
      Give reasons for your answers.   (6 marks)

Task 3.4

Bill Rogers set up a business called Designwise in 1990, designing computer software. As the demand for computers increased dramatically during the 1990s, so the business increased in size to cope with this demand.

In 1995, Bill took on a former colleague as a partner to help run the company. Bill's wife, Helen, also left her job at this time and started to work full time for Designwise as their Administration Director, with an overall responsibility for personnel, accounting and the general office.

Bill retained his job as Chief Designer with responsibility for sales and marketing, while his partner, Henry, became Production Manager. In addition to Bill, Henry and Helen, the present workforce is as follows:

  5 clerks – 2 in Accounts, 2 in the General Office and 1 in Personnel
  3 sales representatives
  1 General Office Manager
  1 Accountant
  1 Sales Manager
  1 Personnel Manager
20 Production workers
  1 Production Supervisor

From the information given above, draw up an organisation chart for the company as it is at the present time.

Task 3.5

The management structure of Docdel plc is shown below:

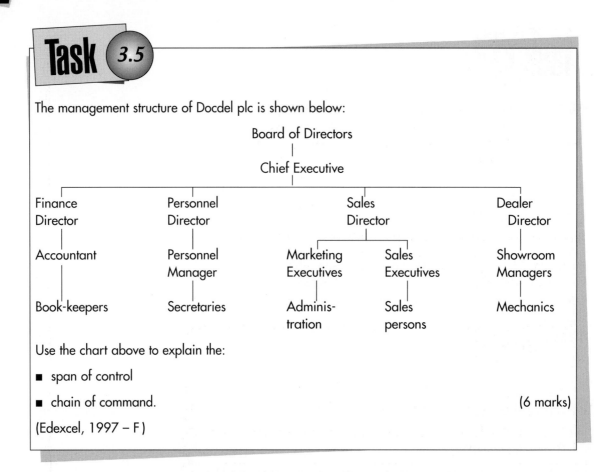

Use the chart above to explain the:

■ span of control

■ chain of command. (6 marks)

(Edexcel, 1997 – F)

EXTERNAL SYSTEMS

We have seen how internal systems operate within a business to aid efficient communication.

We saw in Unit 1 what can happen if communication in a business is poor. Therefore, communication with groups outside of the business is particularly important. These external groups are called **stakeholders** and they are individuals or groups with a direct interest in the business. Managers believe that stakeholders are very important to the success of the business. They think that if the business pays attention to the needs and wants of the different stakeholder groups, this will help the business to succeed.

These are the groups who may be involved in the business or affected by it:

■ suppliers

■ the local community

■ distributors

■ competitors

- financial institutions

- shareholders.

Suppliers

These are businesses who supply other businesses with goods or services. For example, a business producing plastic casings for CDs (the supplier) will supply a company who records the CDs (the customer). If these suppliers receive regular orders and are paid on time, they will provide good-quality products at the required time for the customer.

Suppliers usually build up a good relationship with their customers. They will be interested in the success of their customers because they would want to ensure regular orders for their goods.

Task 3.6

As part of their customer care policy, Docdel plc plan to leave a questionnaire in every car they repair or service.

a) Using the information below and appropriate software, create a customer questionnaire. (8 marks)

> **SERVICE QUESTIONNAIRE**
>
> Prepare a questionnaire for me to be left in clients' cars after service/repairs. I am interested in helpfulness of reception staff, explanations/advice on work done, was invoice detailed enough, quality of work, value for money, cleanliness of car on return. A space for general comments and a space to book next service. Add an opening paragraph and have three levels of response.

b) Explain the advantages of the software you used to create the questionnaire. (6 marks)

(Edexcel, 1997 – H)

The local community

When a business operates within a local community it will try to give something back to that community, by providing jobs or by investing in local schemes.

However, there are some negative aspects. Some businesses can produce goods that can harm the community by producing damaging pollution. The local community will be very concerned about this but if the business tries to reduce the impact it is having on the local environment, this will lead to a better quality of life for everyone and better relations with the local community. Communicating with the local community will ensure these better relations.

Distributors

These are people or businesses who distribute goods, for example an agent who sells the goods of other businesses. This would most likely be a wholesaler. The wholesaler acts as a middleman, generally between the producer and the retailer, who then sells on to the consumer.

Producer ⟶ Wholesaler ⟶ Retailer ⟶ Consumer

This usually means the wholesaler buying large quantities of goods from the producer and breaking them down into the smaller quantities required by the retailer. The other usual services provided by the wholesaler are providing storage of goods and arranging transport of these goods.

Communication between the wholesaler and the producers or retailers is very important because the wholesaler will:

- inform the producers when there is a change in the demand for a particular product so the producers can start manufacturing more or less of those products
- inform retailers of new trends in products so they can stock these new products.

Competitors

These are businesses in the same market, for example mobile phone suppliers, who are trying to gain customers for their products or services. It is said that the more sellers there are in a market, the greater the competition.

Competing businesses will be interested in the competition because they want to become the biggest or most successful business in their market.

The bigger the business is, compared to its competitors, the more it can influence prices.

Financial institutions

Virtually all businesses need to borrow money to start up in business. Many will also need to borrow later to pay for new equipment or to extend their premises. Borrowing money from a **bank** is called a **loan**. The loan is agreed but it has to be paid back with interest within a certain time.

Instead of taking out a loan, some businesses arrange to have an **overdraft** facility instead. This means that they can borrow money from the bank via their current account by spending more than they actually have in the bank. The limit of the overdraft is agreed in advance and must not be exceeded.

Interest rates on overdrafts are higher than that on loans, but the size of the overdraft will vary as money is paid in and out of the account each month. The interest is only calculated on the overdraft for the actual days that the account is overdrawn.

Building societies are also financial institutions, whose main area of activity is to take deposits of money from investors. The building society pays interest on these deposits. They also lend to people and businesses in the form of mortgages, in order to purchase property, usually houses and business premises.

Several building societies have become banks offering a wide range of financial services, such as cheques, credit cards, insurance and estate agencies.

Shareholders

These are the owners of the company. Shareholders purchase shares in a company. Each share owned represents a part of the company. The more shares someone owns, the more of the company belongs to that person.

If the business is successful, the value of the shares will increase. Shareholders should also receive some of the profits that the company makes each year. The part of the profits paid out to shareholders is called the **dividends**. The more profit a company makes, the bigger the dividends. The more shares a person has, the more dividends they receive.

Employees

These are the people who work for a business in return for a wage or salary and they are internal stakeholders. A business will try to improve the working life of its employees by offering them more challenging jobs, better pay and working conditions, as well as greater responsibilities. By doing this, the business will hopefully motivate its employees who will be more committed to the business.

All employees should have contracts of employment, which contain details of their hours of work and other conditions of their employment. These are legal documents setting out the rights and duties of both the employer and the employee.

The contract of employment also contains details of ending the employment, for example in the case of redundancy. This means ending the employment of some employees if there is not enough work, or the job ceases to exist.

Task 3.7

All employees at Docdel plc receive a contract of employment. Explain the importance of this contract to an employee of Docdel plc.

(4 marks)

(Edexcel, 1997 – F and H)

The importance of communicating with all stakeholders

All stakeholders should be kept informed of activities in the business. Communicating with your stakeholders should lead to advantages for the business because:

- providing a better environment for employees to work in helps to recruit and retain employees

- employees will be happy to remain with the business

- shareholders will be more willing to invest in the business

- financial institutions may be more willing to lend to businesses who consider their various stakeholders, as they may be seen as having a more ethical approach to business

- involving all the stakeholder groups should lead to more favourable media coverage with less chance of pressure groups becoming involved with the business.

Revision Questions

1 When a manager asks a subordinate to do a job, this is known as ....
   consultation   delegation   promotion   depreciation

2 Once a job applicant has accepted the job, a .... is drawn up.

   Contract of Employment   Partnership Agreement   data   questionnaire
                                                            capture
                                                            sheet

3 Span of control is the:

   a) number of workers directly controlled by one person
   b) path along which decisions and orders pass
   c) level of authority in a business
   d) terms under which people are employed.

4 The Production Manager at Nocha Ltd has seven employees working under him. This is his:

   a) working environment
   b) financial incentive
   c) profit-sharing
   d) span of control.

5 The levels of authority within Happy Ideas Ltd are its:

   a) chain of command
   b) management structure
   c) hierarchical structure
   d) consultation process.

Task 3.8

The services that Fuller and Brandon Estate Agents provide for its clients require the use of different types of business documentation.

Identify TWO non-financial business forms that Fuller and Brandon would need and explain how each could be used.   (6 marks)

(Edexcel, 1998 – H)

Task 3.9

Gino Nocha has to communicate with:

- customers

- suppliers

- The Ice Cream Alliance (an advisory group for ice cream manufacturers).

Select a different method of communication for each and give your reasons. (8 marks)

(Edexcel, 1999 – F and H)

Extension task

Many employers believe in increased co-operation with their employees and include them in the decision-making process. Employees, in return, must take responsibility for their actions and be flexible.

Assess the effect that this increased co-operation might have on employers and employees. (8 marks)

(Edexcel, 1998 – F and H)

four

COMMUNICATION SYSTEMS

ELECTRONIC

At the end of this unit you should understand what:

▸ telecommunication systems are

▸ a public messaging system is

▸ networks are and how they are used.

TELECOMMUNICATION SYSTEMS

Telecommunication systems enable individuals and businesses to communicate over long distances. They do this by means of telephones, fax machines, pagers, the Internet and video-conferencing.

Telephones

It has become increasingly important for businesses to be able to pass or exchange messages and information immediately. One of the major ways of doing this is by telephone. Using the telephone enables people to contact each other speedily over any distance.

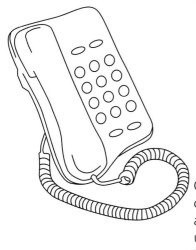

One telephone conversation can deal with both questions and answers and problems can usually be settled immediately. Time spent writing letters is therefore avoided.

A brief telephone call may be cheaper than other methods of communication when we consider the costs involved in, say, producing a letter or an e-mail.

Telephone communication was originally designed for speech but it is now also possible to send digital data via the telephone system. This means that we can send words, files and pictures along the telephone lines, which has led to an increase in electronic communication networks like viewdata. Viewdata is a form of videotex that is accessed using a computer and a modem via the telephone network.

When you are speaking on the telephone you cannot be seen by the other person so he or she cannot see your facial expressions – frowns, smiles etc. Therefore, the way you start and end the call is very important. The tone of your voice is also very important. On most occasions you will be required to sound cheerful, interested, efficient, helpful and polite. You will also have to speak clearly if the person on the other end is taking down details.

When receiving a call you should have a good telephone manner and remain polite at all times – losing your temper achieves nothing!

If you are required to take down a message you must ensure that you take accurate notes that contain all relevant details.

Task 4.1

1   Using any appropriate software, prepare a notice with rules and tips for anyone who has to answer the telephone on behalf of your school.

2   Explain TWO advantages of telephone communication over written communications.   (10 marks)

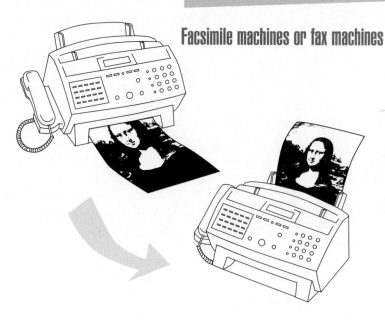

Facsimile machines or fax machines

Faxes are used to send the contents of documents using a telephone line. Text and pictures can be sent. The fax machine at one end scans the document and converts the image into telephone signals. The fax machine at the receiving end prints an exact copy of the document.

The main advantages of using a fax are:

■   high speed when compared with letters

■   hard copy of documents

- the convenience of being able to send text, pictures and images as easily as making a telephone call

- if machines are left on all the time, faxes can be received at any time

- time differences between countries will not be a problem.

There are disadvantages, however:

- faxed printouts are sometimes of poor quality

- the fax machine can sometimes run out of paper at a crucial time

- the telephone connection is sometimes lost.

PC fax software does not need the document to be fed into the fax machine as hard copy. The computer communicates directly with the receiving fax machine. Any faxes received will be stored and then printed as hard copy when needed.

Task 4.2

All Docdel plc dealerships have a fax machine.

State the purpose of a fax machine and explain ONE advantage and ONE disadvantage of its use.   (5 marks)

(Edexcel, 1997 – F)

Pagers

A pager is not connected to the telephone system but the owner of a pager can be contacted to be told when someone is trying to get in touch or that a message is waiting.

In order to page someone, a paging service company is telephoned, this service then sends a signal to the pager. Owners of pagers know when they are trying to be contacted because their pagers beep or vibrate. Pagers also have liquid crystal displays, which can show short messages. They are therefore very useful for contacting people when they are not near telephones.

Some pager users subscribe to services that send information to their pager, such as the latest sports results or stock market details.

Internet

The Internet is a worldwide network of computer systems. Millions of computers are connected by either telephone lines and modems, or cable connections.

Because the telephone network is not yet fully digitised, the digital output of the computer has to be converted to the same analogue form as the telephone. So a device called a **modem** (short for modulator/ demodulator) sits between the computer and the telephone. Modems can be external to the computer but PCs purchased nowadays tend to have modems already installed internally.

There are many organisations that provide access to the Internet and these are known as **Internet Service Providers** (**ISPs**). Some well-known providers are AOL, Demon, Virgin and Yahoo and they usually charge a monthly fee for providing your connection to the Internet. Some ISPs offer free Internet access – Freeserve is one that was started by the electronic retailer Dixons and is now probably the biggest ISP in the UK offering free access.

If you want to explore the Internet, a browser is required and the two most popular are Netscape Navigator and Microsoft Internet Explorer. A browser allows users to search the Internet in an easy and efficient way.

Electronic mail or e-mail

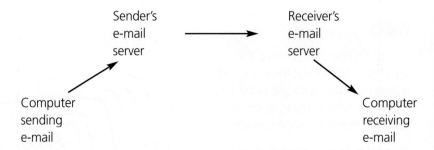

Every user on the Internet has a unique address (for example, liz@hogg.co.uk) just as you have your own home address. By using these e-mail addresses, you can send messages much the same as you would send a letter. E-mail messages are sent from user to user on a computer network, with the message being stored in the recipient's mailbox or inbox. The next time the recipient logs on, they will be told that there is a message waiting, which they can read, print out if they want to and reply to.

Attachments can be sent with e-mails and the same message can be copied to a group of users. You might have your e-mail address at your school or have access at home.

Task 4.3

1 Find out if you have an e-mail address at school.

2 If you have access to e-mail, send a message to a fellow pupil.

3 Try and create an address book of the e-mail addresses of your fellow pupils.

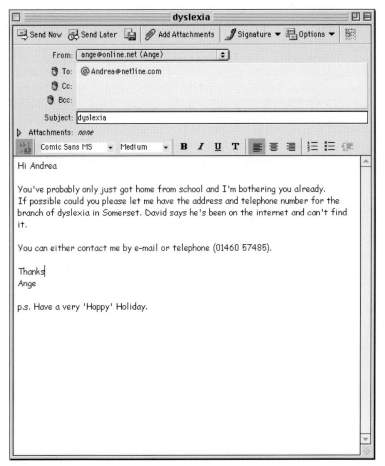

An e-mail message

There are advantages of using e-mail:

■ Speed

- ■ E-mails can reach their destinations instantly, which makes them much faster and more reliable than traditional postal services.

- ■ It also means that there is no uncertainty in knowing precisely when an urgent letter will arrive.

- ■ It is quick and easy to deal with messages – reading letters, sending replies, forwarding copies to others, deleting or filing the messages.

■ Cost

- ■ E-mails will generally be cheaper than ordinary mail because there is no cost for stationery or postage or the hidden costs of a clerk handling the post.

- ■ There should be less paper used because not all e-mails will need to be printed out.

■ Time

- ■ Less time spent on the phone waiting to be put through, finding people unobtainable, holding the line because the number is engaged and leaving messages asking for others to ring back.

■ Flexibility

- ■ Anyone with a PC at home can send and receive messages out of office hours.

- ■ Anyone working away from the office can send and receive messages using a portable computer.

- ■ As with a fax machine, time differences between countries are now not a problem as messages can be sent to await the recipient when he/she logs on.

Disadvantages include:

■ Delay

- ■ If the recipient only logs on once a week then the speed advantage is lost.

- ■ If there is a problem with the recipient's server, you might not know immediately that they haven't received your e-mail.

■ Information overload

- ■ It is sometimes possible to receive dozens of e-mails, which can take a long time to deal with.

- ■ Sometimes important or urgent messages are then overlooked.

- ■ **Junk mail** – just as we receive junk mail through the post, we can receive junk mail via our e-mail.

- ■ **Breakdowns** – sometimes the system is temporarily out of action, which is usually out of our control: the problem could lie with the ISP and is sometimes due to overload on the system, particularly at peak times of the day.

- ■ **Security** – can users be absolutely sure that their confidential message has not been read by a third person with the expertise to break into the system?

Task 4.4

A company, with offices all over the country, decides to introduce electronic mail to link these offices.

1 Explain what is meant by electronic mail.

2 Explain THREE advantages gained by using electronic mail rather than normal postal services.

3 Explain THREE disadvantages of using electronic mail.

4 Give ONE example of when electronic mail would be used instead of using a fax machine.   (16 marks)

Intranet

An Intranet is a network of computers, usually within a company, that uses e-mail and browser software but is not part of the Internet. Employees can use the Intranet to access information related to the company, such as training, social activities, job opportunities, product and company information. It enables employees to share information and is only available to the company's staff.

Video-conferencing

Instead of having to travel to a meeting, managers and executives can go to their company's video-conferencing room (if they have one) or to a centre offering video-conferencing facilities. Certain types of meetings can be replaced by video-conferencing without loss of efficiency.

Video-conferencing enables a meeting to be held through the medium of linked television screens with sound. This means that time is saved because no one is travelling long distances and the cost of the travel is also saved.

A disadvantage, however, is that no matter how good the facilities are, some people prefer a personal meeting because of the concentration needed during a meeting and the valuable role of face-to-face discussion and negotiation.

Task 4.5

Imagine you work for a large company with two sites – one in Middlesbrough and one in Plymouth.

1 When might the managers on both sites use video-conferencing?

2 Explain the advantages of using video-conferencing. (8 marks)

E-commerce

The Internet, together with the reduced cost of telephone calls and the spread of PC ownership, has revolutionised electronic commerce or e-commerce.

E-commerce involves Internet transactions of goods and services to businesses and consumers and can include:

- retail – you can buy virtually anything over the Internet, eg books at www.amazon.co.uk

- travel arrangements – airline and train tickets, hotel bookings and car rental, eg www.lastminute.com

- banking – most banks now allow you to operate your account online, eg www.lloydstsb.co.uk

- many newspapers and magazines offer online versions of their publications, eg www.ft.com

- local schemes selling groceries, eg www.tesco.co.uk

The consumer connects to the online service and can then order goods and pay for these via a credit or debit card. Any goods ordered are delivered by post and it can be very useful for shopping outside normal shop hours and for housebound consumers.

PUBLIC MESSAGING SYSTEMS

If you have ever been in the accident and emergency department of your local hospital or have been waiting in an airport to fly off on your annual holiday or have been waiting for a train, you will have used the public messaging system.

These are electronic noticeboards that keep us informed of, for example, the time we will wait before seeing a doctor or when flights are due to depart and arrive or when trains are due. They are updated frequently and in most cases do away with the need for public announcement systems, which are sometimes very difficult to understand.

NETWORKS

If several computers are linked together, it is called a **network**. Many businesses and schools are networked, which means that they are connected together by cable or high-speed data links.

When computers are linked on the same site, this is called a Local Area Network (LAN) and this is what your school probably has.

When computers are linked over larger areas, they form a Wide Area Network (WAN), which is what a high-street bank has – all the terminals in the different branches will be connected to the bank's head office.

Each user on a network has a user name and password, which are used to log on to the system. There is a Network Manager who is responsible for running and looking after the network.

Local Area Networks (LANs)

Computers in a LAN are connected by cable, which enables the computers to communicate with each other and with other items of hardware, such as printers, which may also be linked to the network. Files of software and data can be passed from one machine to another, e-mail can be used and access to the Internet will be available.

The LAN can be as small as two PCs or may consist of many computers sited in several buildings.

A file server, which is a high-speed workstation with a massive hard disk facility, acts as a central storage device for the whole system.

A printer server controls the printer requirements of all workstations, although sometimes the file server and the printer server will be the same. If you use a network at school, you will know that the printer server controls printing. As each print request is received, it is placed in a queue and once the previous request has been completed, it is printed out.

The advantages of having networked rather than stand-alone machines are:

- resources can be shared – printers, scanners and other expensive pieces of hardware can be shared cutting down on hardware costs
- files of data can be shared allowing all users to use the same data and keep files updated
- programs can be shared – software packages are stored on the file server and downloaded as needed
- users do not need their own disks
- users can access from any workstation but their files cannot be accessed by anyone else

■ all users can access and use the same software at the same time.

Disadvantages of LANs

■ initial cost of purchase and installation can be more than purchasing standalones, but adding extra stations in the future will be cheaper than purchasing extra standalones

■ as more users are connected, the network performance can slow down

■ all computers will be affected if the main cable fails.

LAN organisation

The way networks are designed is sometimes called the architecture or topology and there are three main types – **bus**, **star** and **ring**.

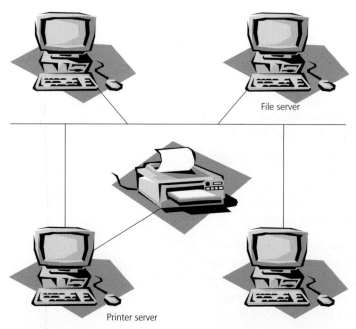

File server

Printer server

A bus network

In a bus network, the workstations, printer server and file server are connected along the central cable. They are easy and inexpensive to install as this system requires the least amount of cable and it is easy to connect new computers. However, a fault centrally will affect all computers and sometimes the network slows down with more users using it.

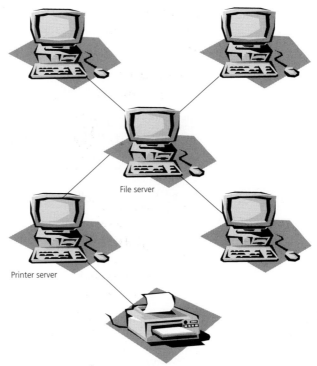

A star network

In a star network, each computer on the network is attached to the central file server. While it is expensive on cabling, it has the advantage that, should a fault occur, it will not affect all computers. Unlike the bus network, the performance of a star network is not affected by the number of computers on the network.

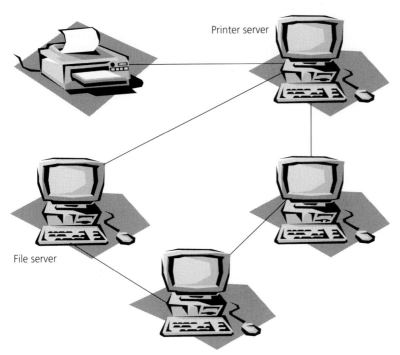

A ring network

In a ring network, each computer is connected to each other in a circular or ring arrangement. Data flowing between computers is fast as it flows in one direction only.

However, it can be difficult to attach new devices to the ring once installed and a cable fault can affect the whole system.

Task 4.6

1 Explain the following terms:

a) file server
b) printer server
c) bus network
d) star network
e) ring network.

2 What reasons might a company have for installing a LAN?

(14 marks)

Wide Area Networks (WANs)

When computers need to be linked over large distances, WANs are used. These can be nationwide or worldwide. Long-distance links are necessary and are provided by the telephone system. British Telecom offer these links, which range from low-speed data links that work over the public telephone system to high-speed data services like the Integrated Services Digital Network (ISDN), which carries voice, data, images and video through a single digital line.

There are two types of WAN – public and private. The best-known public WAN is the Internet, whereas private WANs use privately rented lines.

A WAN needs one or more host computers. Users connect to one host and then can be connected to any other host as required.

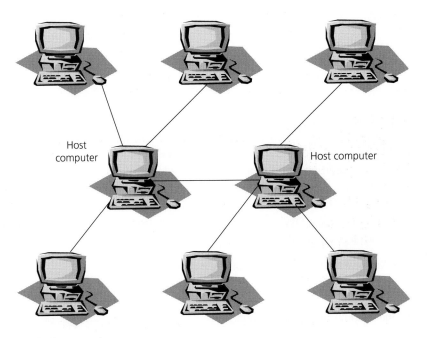

A WAN network

1 If you have a network system in your school, try and interview the Network Manager to find out what his or her job involves.

2 Explain the differences between a LAN and a WAN.

HARDWARE – INPUT DEVICES

Any device used for sending data to the computer is called an **input device**. The input devices you are most likely to see and use are:

- keyboard
- mouse
- joystick
- light pen
- scanner
- touch screen
- bar code reader

- graphics pad

- tracker or roller ball

- digital camera

Keyboard

Most of the data for input to computers still comes in the form of text and is produced using a keyboard. Almost all keyboards follow the same standard layout which is the same as an ordinary typewriter but with extra keys for functions you cannot do on the typewriter. This standard layout is called the QWERTY layout and comes from the top six keys on the left hand side of the keyboard.

The keyboard is divided into four main areas:

- the alphabet keys

- the function keys across the top

- numeric keys across the top and in the numeric keypad

- cursor keys and other keys used for editing.

The keyboard is a very reliable means of inputting text and every computer comes with a keyboard. It is suitable for a range of applications from word processing documents, entering customer or client details into a database and entering figures into a spreadsheet.

However because not everyone using a keyboard is experienced and accurate, errors can be made with copying the data and it can be time-consuming if the operator is not quick. In addition, if the person entering the data does this for long periods throughout the day they could suffer repetitive strain injury (RSI). This is a condition which affects wrists in particular and is very painful. It can stop the operator from doing quite ordinary tasks like holding a cup or writing.

Mouse

A mouse is a device which lets you control the movement of the cursor on the screen. It has one, two or three buttons which are clicked. You will have heard people saying 'double click on the icon' which means clicking with the mouse.

As well as a standard mouse you can get a cordless mouse which enables you to use the mouse from a distance of up to 2 metres away from the computer. It uses digital radio technology and could be used for presenting a lesson or talk with an electronic whiteboard. The teacher or speaker may prefer to walk around the room and operate the mouse from different places in the room and not be confined to standing at the front all of the time.

The advantages of using a mouse are:

■ they are inexpensive to buy

■ they are easy to use and can be used by right or left handed people

■ when selecting from the screen they can be quicker than using the keyboard

■ it is quite difficult to use a computer without using a mouse.

However

■ short cut keys can be quicker than a mouse if the user is experienced in using these

■ it is not easy to make accurate drawings using a mouse.

Joystick

If you own a computer and play games you will probably use a joystick. The lever on the joystick operates the object on the screen. Think of your computer games – what objects does the joystick operate?

Light pen

A light pen is a pen-shaped input device which enables the user to select a point on the screen. It does this by sensing the presence or absence of light. They are used in supermarkets to read bar codes (see Unit 10). They are also used with a CAD (computer aided design) package. The main advantage of using a light pen and a CAD package is it is more accurate than a mouse because you can point at the option that you want.

Scanner

A scanner can be used to input typed, handwritten and graphical material into the computer. The scanner scans the material and OCR software can be used so text can be word processed. Diagrams and pictures or photographs can be altered by loading them into graphics software.

The scanner you are most familiar with is probably the flatbed scanner. It works a bit like a photocopier. The document to be scanned is placed face down on the scanner and a sensor scans or reads the document.

A more expensive and versatile scanner is the sheet-feed scanner. It is capable of scanning a variety of documents. It is useful in any business because it is quicker at scanning black and white documents than a flatbed scanner and it can cope with more than one document at a time.

Touch screen

A touch screen allows the user to enter data by just touching the screen. The user does not have to use a keyboard. You have probably seen these in McDonalds, your local library or even your dining hall at school if you use swipe cards to buy your lunch.

The main advantages of a touch screen are:

- no extra items of hardware are needed

- in a place like McDonalds where the users' hands get greasy, having a touch screen means the mouse or keyboard do not get dirty

- because the same information is being used all the time, the touch screen speeds up input.

The main disadvantage of a touch screen is that the user can only select data from the screen, no other data can be entered.

Bar code reader

There are bar codes on nearly everything we buy. These bar codes contain a great deal of information which help managers and others in business keep up-to-date with what products are selling. The managers can then make decisions on where to place goods in the shop to try and increase sales and what products perhaps need to be withdrawn from sale.

Bar codes are not however used only in retailing. They can be used in:

- medicine to identify blood and tissue samples and on patient records

- in banking, particularly on cheques and cheque books

- libraries use bar codes to record books borrowed and returned

A bar code sanner or reader is used to read the bar code and record data. The reader can look like a light pen (mentioned earlier) or it can look like a hand-held scanner and once it has read the bar codes these are passed to the computer which holds all product details in a large data file.

Graphics pad

A graphics pad is used to draw with a stylus on to a touch sensitive surface. As the user draws the image appears on the screen. The user can place paper on the touch sensitive surface and use a pen or pencil which makes it very useful for tracing maps and diagrams.

Tracker or roller ball

A tracker ball is like an upside down mouse. You move a mouse around but with a tracker ball, the whole device stays still and you only move the tracker ball. Unlike a mouse it does not need a large flat surface but like a mouse it has the function buttons.

You will probably have seen tracker balls built into portable computers. this is because if you are using your portable computer away from a desk – perhaps on the train or on your knee while you are watching television – you would not be able to use a mouse. The tracker ball then lets you move the cursor around the screen and select from menus exactly as you would if you were using a mouse.

Digital camera

A digital camera looks very similar to an ordinary camera but pictures taken with a digital camera are stored in the computer memory rather than on film. A digital camera lets you see the picture before you take it which means if you do not like it you can choose not to take it.

The pictures are displayed on screen and can be imported into graphics or art packages for editing.They are printed on special photographic paper which means they look no different from photographs taken with a traditional camera – sometimes they are better!

OUTPUT DEVICES

An output devices lets you see the results of the computer's operations. The most common output devices are visual display units (VDU), printers and plotters.

Visual display unit or monitor

A VDU or monitor is a screen which lets you see what you are doing with your computer. They come in different sizes – 15", 17", 19" and 21" and you measure the size of the screen from corner to corner.

Monitors look like televisions, you can now get flat screen monitors which take up less space than traditional monitors but which are still relatively expensive to buy.

The clarity of the image on the monitor is determined by how many pixels the image is made up of. A pixel is a tiny dot and if you look closely at your monitor you will see these pixels. The more pixels per square centimetre of screen the better the image you will get.

Portable computers use liquid crystal displays because they are much lighter and use much less power than conventional monitors.

Printers

In order to produce a permanent copy of anything you have created on screen you would use a printer to give you a hard copy.

- Dot matrix printer

A dot matrix printer is known as an impact printer because the print head travels across the paper and the pins in the print head strike the paper. They are used to print multiple copies of pre-printed forms which usually come as continuous stationery – businesses use these to print out invoices and other financial documents.

The advantages of using dot matrix printers are:

- they are cheap to buy and their running costs are low

- they are very reliable and can be used in dirty work environments

- because they use continuous stationery they are useful in businesses where many copies of documents are printed out, for example in a business which issues invoices.

- they are versatile because most of them can print in condensed, standard and enlarged mode.

The disadvantages of dot matrix printers are:

- the quality of print is not as good as that of an ink jet or laser printer

- to get near letter quality (NLQ) print, the words are printed twice which makes them slower than ink jet or laser printers

- they are noisy which in an office can be very distracting and irritating.

- Ink jet printers

An ink jet printer is a non-impact printer which can produce printouts nearly as good as laser printers. They use liquid ink to spray characters on to a page which is what provides the good quality print.

Their advantages are:

- they are compact so do not take up too much room

- they are quiet – quieter than a dot matrix printer

- they are relatively cheap to buy – what prices have you seen for ink jet printers?

Their disadvantages are:

- they are slow in comparison to a laser printer especially if text, graphics and colour are used

- care should be taken when printing because the ink will be wet and liable to smudge.

- Laser printer

A laser printer is another non-impact printer and since their prices have been dropping are becoming increasingly popular. They work very much like a photocopier using toner which is transferred to the page and fused with heat.

Their advantages are:

– they produce very high quality printouts

– they are fast – faster than laser and dot matrix printers

– they are quiet – in fact they are virtually silent

Their disadvantages are:

– their cost which can run into thousands of pounds, though their prices have been dropping

– the toner which can be expensive – more expensive than ink jet cartridges.

Plotters

A plotter is an output device used for producing high quality graphical output particularly line drawings such as building plans and electronic circuits. They are either pen plotters or penless plotters.

A pen plotter uses pens which move across the paper to draw images. These are cheaper than penless plotters and probably what you use in school in the Technology Department.

A penless plotter is used when high densities are needed for example, in printed circuit boards, machines and machine parts.

Speakers

Computers have an internal speaker which beeps at you when you press a wrong key or when you press two keys together. However, multimedia computers bought nowadays have external speakers which allow you to listen to music from CDs or music from the Internet.

Task 4.8

The introduction of information technology to Harbon Estates Ltd is being planned by the directors. The setting up of a network in their offices will raise a number of issues which include types of hardware.

Advise the directors of Harbon Estates Ltd as to the advantages and/disadvantages of the following types of printer:

■ dot matrix

■ inkjet

■ laser.   (8 marks)

(adapted from Edexcel, 1998 – H)

STORAGE DEVICES

When you are using the computer, any data, information or files are stored in the computer's memory. However, the memory does not save this data, information and files when the computer is switched off so we use disks and disk drives to do this. These saved files may be valuable and very important to the business and impossible to replace so it is important to ensure they are secure when they are saved (see Unit 17).

Your computer or the computers at school will probably have one hard disc drive which is called the C drive, one floppy drive which is called the A drive, as well as a CD-ROM drive which is called the D drive.

The hard drive is where all the applications software is kept. It is like a filing cabinet and we measure the size of these in gigabytes (GB). A typical computer size is 1 GB which is capable of holding the operating system, for example Microsoft Windows. What is the GB of your computer if you have one?

The hard disk is exactly what it says – a hard, round device which rotates at high speed and which is capable of storing lots of data. The hard disks are protected in sealed drives so that no dirt or dust can damage them.

The floppy drive is designed to accept 3½" disks. This makes floppy disks very useful for transferring data and information between computers. Do you transfer disks between your home computer and your school computers? They are also used for back-up of files as a security measure.

Floppy disks can store up to 1.4 MB of data which is approximately 300 A4 pages of text. If graphics are saved then not as much can be saved on a floppy disk.

Floppy disks can be write-protected so nothing can be erased from the disk accidentally. However data can be lost from the disk by keeping them too near magnetic fields, for example televisions. Data can also be lost through someone touching the surface of the disk or damage to the disk caused by liquids or generally not looking after disks by not keeping them stored properly in a disk box.

Zip disks are slightly larger and thicker than floppy disks and can hold 100MB or 250MB of data which is considerably more than a floppy disk. However they need their own zip drives.

The CD-ROM drive (compact disk drive read only memory) is used to read from the disk only and not write or store data. A typical CD-ROM holds approximately 650 MB of data which is about 450 1.4 MB floppy disks.

However CD writers are now available which let you store programs and data on to the disk so they too can be used as a storage device.

Revision Questions

1 What enables computers to be linked by telephone? ....

laptop computer   modem   light pen   scanner

2 If Louisa Designs uses e-mail to communicate, this means ....

computer to   express post   using telex   using tannoy
computer

3 A computer that is not linked to other computers is ....

networked   a standalone   a modem   a WAN

4 What would enable the office to contact the Showroom Manager when he is in another part of the business? ....

laptop   fax   pager   printer

5 Docdel plc links its 41 dealerships together with a ....

network   computer   database   spreadsheet

6 The Harbon Estates Ltd surveyor keeps in contact with his Head Office through his laptop computer and ....

teletext   telex   e-mail   surface mail

7 Fuller and Brandon has three standalone computers. A secretary would use one of the following to transfer files from one computer to another ....

a) hard disk and CD-ROM   b) floppy disk and 'a' drive
c) CD-ROM and 'd' drive   d) hard disk and 'c' drive

8 If Nocha Ltd had a computer network, all users would need authorised entry. They would be given a ....

modem   password   laptop   calculator

9 Which of the following describes a standalone computer? ....

a) linked to a network   b) not connected to any other computer
c) can be used without a mouse or keyboard d) can be used by a number of people at the same time

10 Data flowing between computers in a .... network is fast as it only flows in one direction.

star   ring   bus   wide area

11 A mouse is ....

an input device   a system   an output device   a network

12 An example of an output device is a ....

light pen   screen   mouse   bar code reader

13 Each Docdel plc dealership produces a brochure of second hand cars. An image of some cars is included by using a ....

scanner   plotter   modem   mouse

14 Nocha Ltd uses different types of printer. The .... printer gives the best quality output.

laser   dot matrix   inkjet   bubble jet

15 Data on members of Happy Ideas Ltd Collectors Club is processed by a ....

computer   keyboard   mouse   VDU

16 The printer at Happy Ideas Ltd with the lowest output quality is the ....

daisy wheel   inkjet   dot matrix   laser

Task 4.9

Harbon Estates Ltd, the property development company, only has one computer. The directors of Harbon Estates Ltd want to make more use of information technology but they do not understand the difference between a network system and standalone machines.

1 Explain what is meant by:

a) a network system
b) standalone machines. (4 marks)

2 Recommend to Harbon Estates Ltd either a network system or standalone machines and give reasons for your choice.
(5 marks)

(Edexcel, 1999 – H)

Task 4.10

Sam Stephens uses information technology to run the Collectors Club. The club has over 3000 members worldwide. Sam is the first point of contact for club members. She also deals with queries from the agents in seven countries.

Her basic hardware configuration is:

- a standalone computer
- a printer
- a fax
- a modem.

Explain what a modem is and how it helps Sam to run the Collectors Club. (8 marks)

(Edexcel, 2000 – H)

Task 4.11

In order to improve administration at Happy Ideas Ltd, the directors are purchasing computers and software. The computers will also have monitors and keyboards.

Explain the purpose of each and say whether it is an input or output device. (4 marks)

(Edexcel, 2000 – F)

Task 4.12

Explain how each piece of hardware listed below might be used at Louisa Designs.

scanner   light pen   plotter   laptop computer
(8 marks)

(Edexcel, 1996 – F)

Task 4.13

Employees of Nocha Ltd use different input devices when working on computers.

Consider the advantages and disadvantages of using a mouse as an input device. (6 marks)

(Edexcel, 1999 – F)

Task 4.14

Laura Hughes has the responsibility for training staff in the use of information technology at Nocha Ltd. She feels that a handbook for staff is needed.

Explain how Laura would use both input and output devices to produce a page of the handbook that contains text, graphics and tables. (6 marks)

(Edexcel, 1999 – H)

Extension task

Laura Hughes is unsure whether to recommend the installation of standalone or networked computers to the directors. She asks you to help her make a recommendation to the directors.

Prepare a short **report** for Laura Hughes in which you compare stand-alone machines with a LAN and give a recommendation with your reasons. (14 marks)

(Edexcel, 1999 – H)

COMMUNICATION SYSTEMS

WORD PROCESSING

At the end of this unit you should understand:

▸ the facilities of word processing.

Word processing (see Unit 2 – Paper based systems) allows you to edit, format and produce documents. It is used for a wide variety of tasks, such as:

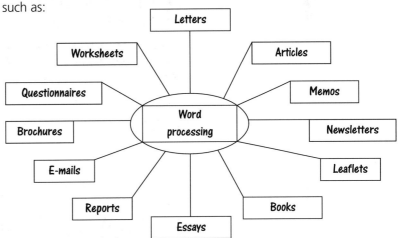

The following definitions should help you to develop your knowledge of the facilities that a word processing package can offer you. Can you use all of them efficiently and effectively?

WORD PROCESSING FACILITIES

Amend

To amend means to change or adjust whatever you have keyed in. For example, if you have made an error or have misspelt something. You can take the cursor (flashing point on the screen) to the character after the error and press the 'backspace' key, or take the cursor to the point before the character to be deleted and press the 'Delete' key.

The test has an error.
(Test needs changing to text)

Borders

Borders can make a piece of work more interesting and effectively display the task set. You can put borders around a sentence, paragraph, section or whole document. The thickness and the colour of the border can also be decided. There are a variety of variations on borders, such as 3-D ones or ones you have created yourself. Borders can be made up of lines or even simple graphics, with the size being altered to fit whatever you want.

A border has been placed around this sentence.

Centre

Centring is part of the term justification, where you can choose how the lines of the page look. To centre a line means to have each line balanced in the centre of the page. There are a variety of ways to centre your work – check the ways your particular program allows you to centre.

This line is centred.

Copy

To copy is to repeat either a sentence, paragraph or phrase as many times as you want. There are a variety of ways your program will allow you to do it. Check which you find the easiest. Highlight the work you want and then 'copy' it and 'paste' it somewhere else. Remember to adjust the spacing after you have copied the work. The chorus of a song is normally copied at the end of each verse.

Drawing

Drawing enables you to put a variety of different shapes and sizes onto your work without actually using a special graphics package. An example of this is labelling a diagram – lines can be drawn from points on the diagram to their labels. Bubble diagrams or mind maps are also an example of where drawing could be used.

Edit

You can edit (sometimes known as amend), your work by changing what you have keyed in. Editing can be classed as deleting, inserting, moving etc of text. You should edit your work after you have proofread it, to make sure that it reads correctly and that there are no errors.

Enter

To enter can mean to actually key in text, numbers or characters onto the screen. It can also mean to press the 'Enter' key. This takes your cursor onto the next line.

Find and replace

Find and replace is a useful tool when you want to search in your work for a word or phrase and then replace it with another one. An example of this could be if you are updating a letter or piece of text that was written in the year 1999. We are now in the next century, so for a piece of work to be up-to-date, you would want all references to 1999 changed to 2001. You would use the 'find and replace' facility to find every date containing 1999 and replace it with 2001. This feature can be used for phrases as well as numbers and words.

Fonts

An extremely useful tool for displaying your work. You can change the size and style of your writing for every single word if you want to. It enables you to have headings with a fancy style of writing. The font size can be changed to ensure that the work fits in the space you have available. Examples are given below:

This is Arial type.

This is called Chicago.

This is Copperplate.

This is One Stroke Script – typed in size 16.

Footer

A footer is something that is placed at the end of each page of work. It can be examples of where you have had your source of information from, it can be your actual name, in fact anything you wish could appear at the end of every page. Footers will often contain the page number, which of course will change as the pages change, for example. Newcastle\events\GNVQ – 30 March 2000-doc

Format

Formatting is changing the look of the text or the way in which the work is presented. For example, you can format work so that all the headings are in bold. Other examples are:

to format the text into bullet points like this

- **to place text in columns.**

Function keys

Function keys are a way of increasing the speed with which you operate the computer. Various programs have different function keys. For example, pressing F8 highlights text, the more you press it the more it highlights. You can then change the way the text is presented, you can delete, put into italics, underline etc. Learn the function keys as they help you to speed up the use of the computer.

Grammar

Many modern programs, such as Word, have facilities such as a grammar check. This means that, as you are keying in your work, a green wavy line may appear underneath what you have keyed in. If this happens, the program is letting you know that you may have made a grammatical error, which should be checked. Grammar checks are very useful if your own English is not very good. However, sometimes the suggestions made have faults, for example, they could have been written by an American or they could have analysed your work wrongly as the English language is very complicated. You will need to exercise care when using this facility.

Graphs

Graphs can normally be copied and added to the text you are keying in. Most programs allow you to copy and paste graphs into any word processed text. For specific ways, check the program you are using.

Headers

A header is very similar to a footer, except that it comes at the top of the page instead of the bottom. In this case, you are more likely to want a reference to what the text is about, for example, Chapter One could be at the top of each page. Your name is another example.

Images

Images are photos, diagrams etc that can either be scanned into the document or copied and pasted.

Import

Importing is bringing in text or diagrams from one program into another. One example is the importing of clip art from a program into a word processing document. This is usually used to improve the appearance of your work.

An example of clip art

Insert

To insert is to enter text, numbers or characters into your word processed document. You can also insert whole documents, as well as pictures etc.

Justification

Justification is the way that the text is spread over each line. Full justification spreads the text evenly to ensure that all lines of text end exactly at the right-hand margin. This creates a straight margin and gives the work a professional look, such as in newspapers and magazines. Lines of text can also have left justification, which means that they line up only at the left, or right justification, where they line up only at the right, like your address at the top right of a letter.

> This is an example of justified text, which inserts extra spaces between the words to make sure that each line is exactly the same length and the left-hand margin is straight.

> This is an example of right justified text, where the right hand margin is straight.

Mail merge

Mail merge is the process of combining names and addresses stored in a data file with a main document in a separate file, to give the impression that an individual document has been sent. In this way, by merging a standard letter with a customer's personal details, completely personalised letters can be printed out automatically for all customers. This is often called a mailshot. Your school might use mail merge to communicate with parents.

The standard letter is produced with field names and these are replaced with the information from those fields in the data file during the merge. An example of the beginning of a standard letter is shown below.

> 30 January 2001
>
> <FirstName> <LastName>
> <Company>
> <Address1>
> <Town>
> <Postcode>
>
> Dear <FirstName>

Margins

Margins are the blank spaces between the edge of the text and the edge of a page. When you open a word processing document, the margins on the left and right and the top and bottom of the page will be automatically set. You can use these pre-set margins or you may need to set wider/narrower ones to give particular effects or to improve layout. Margins can be set for an entire document or a specific section. See the example below that shows different margins for specific sections.

> The default margin setting for Word documents is 1.25 inches on the left and right and 1 inch at the top and bottom of the page.
>
> To set new margins you drag the margin boundaries on the rulers.

Move

The move function means that a block of text can be moved to another part of the document. This allows changes to be made and might include moving sentences or paragraphs from one position to another. It is also useful when you are composing documents as it allows you to experiment with sentence and paragraph order.

Overwrite

The overwrite mode allows you to replace existing text as you type. This saves you having to delete the text you do not want – you simply type over it.

Page setup

The page setup function allows you to change the way that your pages look. You can change your margins and your paper size. You can also choose the orientation of your page – portrait orients the page vertically (taller than it is wide), landscape orients the page horizontally (wider than it is tall).

Portrait

Landscape

Pagination

Word processing packages automatically put in page breaks when you type more than can fit on an A4 page. However, there are many occasions when you will want to choose your own page breaks before your text reaches the bottom of the page. Using the page break function allows you to do this.

Paste

Paste works with 'copy'. It enables you to put or paste text into various places in your document. First of all, you copy the text you want to move, then you paste it into a different position. You can paste the same material over and over again, for example, the chorus in a hymn or song.

Proofreading

This means checking your work on the screen to identify any errors before you print it. You should check for keyboarding errors, spelling mistakes, missing words, incorrect line spacing, wrong spacing after punctuation marks etc. These should be corrected before your work is printed out. It is also important to check the printed copy for errors that may have escaped your notice on the screen.

Spellcheck

A spellcheck will look in its dictionary for each word you have put in your document. For those it cannot find, it will suggest alternative spellings. However, it should be remembered that a spellcheck does not solve all problems, for instance there may be two different spellings of a word and you will need to know which one is correct in the context of your work.

Styles

The style function allows you to set different styles for your work, such as varying fonts, alignment and sizes. You can save all these varying styles and select which you wish to use for the document or for different sections within one document.

Tab

When you press the 'Tab' key, the cursor moves across the line to different positions. Tab stops are pre-set positions across the page which can be changed. They are useful when setting out tables and figures in a document. The position of the tab stops is shown on the horizontal ruler line above the document.

Template

A template is a special document that stores text, styles, formatting, macros and page information as a framework for use in other documents. Templates are used for a range of commercial documents, such as business letters, memos, invoices and newsletters.

Thesaurus

If you need help in finding exactly the right word to use, the Thesaurus can assist you. If you highlight a word in a document, the Thesaurus will list words with similar meanings (called synonyms). This saves you time and improves the quality and readability of your document.

WordArt

This function allows you to add interest to your documents by changing your text. You can stretch it, resize it, reshape it and even rotate it. It is a great way to enhance a newsletter or flyer. You can see an example to the right.

Task 5.1

1 Word process the following notice, which will appear in the local newspaper. Remember to use as many facilities as you can to make the notice attractive and appealing.

   JUMBLE WANTED
   For Baverstock Foundation School and Specialist College

   we will be collecting on 7 June 2001

   OUR JUMBLE SALE
   will be held at

   BECKETT'S FARM
   Algester Road
   Wythall

   On Saturday 15 June 2001

   Doors open at 1430 hours

   Come early for the biggest bargains

2 Recall the task and centre the work. Use different fonts for the most important parts and emphasise certain headings by giving them extra spacing. Remember you not only have different fonts, but bold, underscore and capital letters to display your work.

Task 5.2

You work as a Personal Assistant to Louisa Phillips and she is going to Newcastle-upon-Tyne. She wants you to book overnight accommodation for her. She has left these notes for you. The hotel is The Vermont Hotel, Eldon Square, Newcastle-upon-Tyne, NE34 5DT

(10 marks)

Can you book me the following please:

Arriving   *One night*
on 28 October   *only*

Single room with bath

Non-smoking room
please   *An evening*
                                                      meal — at 8.30.

(Edexcel, 1996 – H)

Task 5.3

Using suitable software, prepare a letter for signature by Nick Dunn, Showroom Manager, inviting customers to view a new car model. Use the notes left for you by Nick Dunn. The showroom address is Docdel plc, 20 The High, Houghton-le-Spring, SR7 9TD.
Tel: 01963 213974
Fax: 01963 267777

(9 marks)

Leave a space for the address.

Launch of new Lexus model — Friday (insert an appropriate date).
From 6.30 pm at Jesmond Street. Refreshments will be available.
They can book a test drive. Everyone attending will be entered in a
draw for two tickets for the 200- Grand Prix. Sales staff will be on
hand to discuss new purchases and our finance people can explain the
various option for borrowing money etc.

Nick —

(Edexcel, 1997 – F and H)

Task 5.4

Mr Roger George of 2 Middle Lane, Hart Village, TS24 2VN wants to sell his house through Fuller and Brandon. He rang to enquire. Design a letterhead for Fuller and Brandon and prepare a letter to Mr George thanking him for his telephone call. Tell him that you are sending a form with this letter. He must complete the form and return it. Fuller and Brandon's address is Deacon's Chambers, 19 Pantiles, Waterlooville, Hants, PO32 9WC

Tel: 01254 328719   Fax: 01254 558831   (10 marks)

(Edexcel, 1998 – F)

Revision Questions

1 Amending your work means .... what you have keyed in.

   copying   changing   finding   drawing

2 Find and .... is a tool that lets you search in your work for a word
   and then replace it with another one.

   enter   overwrite   insert   replace

3 You can change the size and style of your writing by changing the ....

   image   colour   font   paint

4 .... keys help you to increase the speed with which you operate
   the computer.

   function   formatting   planning   set-up

5 .... appear at the top of the page and ....
   at the bottom.

   margins   headers   paragraphs   footers

6 Justification means that you have a .... right and left margin.

   ragged   centred   straight   wavy

7 The process of combining a data file of names and addresses with a standard letter is called
   ....

   inserting   mail-merge   formatting   grammar-check

8 The .... mode allows you to replace existing text as you type.

   entry   overwrite   underwrite   overscore

9 .... are pre-set positions across the page.

   margins   tab stops   rulers   edges

10 You should always .... your work on the screen to identify any
   errors before you print it.

   move   paste   proof-read   copy

Extension task

1 Copy the following passage, spellcheck it, save it as Passage 1 and then print a copy.

Mail merge means merging a list of names and addresses held in a database with a standard letter to create personalised letters. In this way, the same letter (apart from the personal details) can be sent to a number of people. For example, it is useful for the owners of businesses who want to mail all their customers to let them know about a new product or service. It saves spending a great deal of time changing personal information and gives the impression that each customer has been sent an individual document.

The steps to creating a mail merge are:

- prepare the letter containing the unchanging information and the merge fields for the personal information

- create the database of personal information to fit into the merge fields

- merge the two.

2 Recall the passage and justify it, change the margins to give a wider left-hand margin, add the title Mail Merge using WordArt and change the bullet points to numbers. Save your work again, calling the file Passage2 and print out a copy.

SIX

COMMUNICATION SYSTEMS

SPREADSHEETS

At the end of this unit you should understand:

▶ what a spreadsheet is

▶ what spreadsheets are used for

▶ what graphs and charts are used for.

You should also be able to:

▶ create your own spreadsheet

▶ create formulae to add, subtract, multiply and divide

▶ create and use a 'what if' spreadsheet

▶ construct graphs and charts from a spreadsheet.

WHAT IS A SPREADSHEET?

Spreadsheets can be used for any work involving numerical data because they present the data in columns and rows, looking like a grid of squares. Spreadsheets not only display the data but they can also manipulate the data. This means that a spreadsheet can do the calculations for you, which saves time. Examples of some of the uses of spreadsheets are:

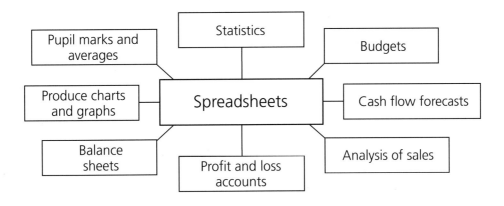

Spreadsheets are used in businesses to speed up the process of doing a variety of calculations. Now let us see what a spreadsheet looks like and how it works.

HOW SPREADSHEETS WORK

A page of a spreadsheet looks like a grid of squares, known as cells. This grid is labelled A, B, C, D, E etc along the top from left to right – these represent the **columns** that go down the page. At the left-hand side, the grid is labelled 1, 2, 3, 4, 5, etc down the page – these represent the **rows** going across the page.

The diagram below is only a small part of what a spreadsheet can look like. In some businesses they can be pages and pages long.

	A	B	C	D	E	F
1	*					
2						
3						
4						
5						
6						

When referring to a spreadsheet we often use what is called '**Cell Referencing**' and it is important to understand what is meant by this. It means that each cell has a particular reference number or label, for example, **A1** is a cell in column **A** and in row **1**. It is similar to playing the game 'Battleships' or looking for a road on a street map. When using cell referencing you always give the column first before the row. A1 cell is shown by the * in the diagram above.

So you can see that cell referencing is very important when you want to enter formulae into a spreadsheet or refer to a particular cell.

You can enter the following types of information into cells on a spreadsheet:

- Words – eg titles, headings of rows and columns

- Numbers – eg calculations, currency and dates

- Formulae – so that calculations can be performed.

One of the main reasons for using a spreadsheet is that it acts like a calculator. Because you put in formulae to tell the spreadsheet what to do with the numbers you have entered, it works out the answers for you in a fraction of the time it would take with a calculator or a pen and paper.

When using a spreadsheet for the first time, a number of people might use a calculator to carry out the calculations or might even try and work them out in their head. This may be fine for small spreadsheets but will certainly cause problems and many mistakes if you are working on a large spreadsheet. We will look at some of the simple functions that a spreadsheet can do for you if you use a formula.

Addition

Look at the example given below. It shows how a person could be spending their pocket money in one week.

	A	B	C	D	E
1	**Bus fare**	**10.00**			
2	**Sweets**	**4.75**			
3	**Presents**	**6.99**			
4	**Clothes**	**19.89**			
5	**Sundries**	**8.00**			
6	**Total**				

Task 6.1

Open a spreadsheet and enter only the data shown in bold above.

Suppose you wanted to add up the amount of money spent in that week. First of all you would put your cursor into the cell where you want the total to go, ie B6. Then key in the following formula:

=SUM(B1:B5)
Then press enter.

This will tell the spreadsheet to add up all the numbers in the cells between B1 and B5 and put the answer in B6. (The spreadsheet you use may start a formula with a different character, for example, @. Check which one your spreadsheet uses.)

The other way of doing this would be to key in the following: B1+B2+B3+B4+B5, but the first formula is far simpler and quicker to use.

Task 6.2

Enter the formula =SUM(B1:B5) into cell B6 and press enter. This should give you the total £49.63.

One of the advantages of using a formula for addition is that, if you then have to change a number in one of the cells, the total figure will automatically be changed, saving you extra work. If you look at the diagram below, you will see that the amount for presents has been changed to £3.99 and the total has automatically adjusted to £46.63.

	A	B	C	D	E
1	Bus fare	10.00			
2	Sweets	4.75			
3	Presents	3.99			
4	Clothes	19.89			
5	Sundries	8.00			
6	Total	46.63			

Task 6.3

Type £3.99 in cell B3 and press enter. You will see that a new total has appeared in cell B6.

Subtraction

Just as you can easily add cells together you can also subtract them. Another simple formula is used.

In the task we are doing, suppose you wish to subtract the cost of the clothes from the total.

Task 6.4

Type the following formula in cell B7=B6–B4 and press enter. This will give you the Total minus the cost of the clothes.

Add 'A' to the word 'Total' in cell A6 so that it reads Total A. Type Total B in cell A7.

Your Total B should be £26.74 and your spreadsheet should look like the one shown over the page.

	A	B	C	D	E
1	Bus fare	10.00			
2	Sweets	4.75			
3	Presents	3.99			
4	Clothes	19.89			
5	Sundries	8.00			
6	Total A	46.63			
7	Total B	26.74			

Multiplication

Now let us try multiplication. Again, to multiply figures you only have to enter a different formula and the spreadsheet will do it all for you.

If you wanted to find out exactly how much is spent on sweets throughout the year, you would key the following formula into cell B8:

=B2*52
Then press enter.

The B2 is the cell reference for the amount of money spent on sweets each week, the star represents the multiply sign and 52 of course is the number of weeks in the year.

Task 6.5

Put your cursor in cell B8, enter the formula =B2*52 and press enter.

Type Total C in cell A8.

Your Total C should be 247.00 and your spreadsheet should look like the one over the page.

	A	B	C	D	E
1	Bus fare	10.00			
2	Sweets	4.75			
3	Presents	3.99			
4	Clothes	19.89			
5	Sundries	8.00			
6	Total A	46.63			
7	Total B	26.74			
8	Total C	247.00			

We now have 3 different totals showing you how to add — subtract — multiply —

Division

Dividing an amount is also very easy to do in a spreadsheet. If you want to see how much is spent on sweets each day you would enter the following formula:

=B2/7
Then press enter.

Remember, so that the program knows you are using a formula the equals sign is always used first.

In this formula, B2 represents the amount spent on sweets in a week and the solidus (divide sign) tells it to divide this by 7, which is the number of days.

Task 6.6

Enter the following formula in cell C2 of your spreadsheet =B2/7 and press enter.

Your answer should be 0.68 and your spreadsheet should look like the one over the page.

	A	B	C	D	E
1	Bus fare	10.00			
2	Sweets	4.75	0.68		
3	Presents	3.99			
4	Clothes	19.89			
5	Sundries	8.00			
6	Total A	46.63			
7	Total B	26.74			
8	Total C	247.00			

The daily total for sweets is shown here

Task 6.7

Save your spreadsheet and call it Pocket Money. Print a copy of your spreadsheet.

These are the four main mathematical operations that you will have to carry out, so just to remind you of the signs you use:

Operation	Sign
To add two numbers	+
To add more than two numbers	= SUM (D9:D13)
To subtract numbers	−
To multiply numbers	*
To divide numbers	/

And remember every formula begins with = or whatever character you have to use for your software.

Although these are the most commonly used types of formula, a spreadsheet also allows you to carry out other functions, such as finding out averages, percentages, the maximum and minimum of a set of numbers etc.

Now we will look at some of the other features of spreadsheets, which you may need to use.

Autosum

When you want to add together a range of numbers in a spreadsheet, instead of working out the formula to give you the total, you can use the autosum function.

- Put your cursor in the cell where you want your total to appear.
- Click on the autosum button on the toolbar – the button looks like this Σ.
- A formula will appear in the cell.
- Press Enter, and this will change to the total.

Autocalculate

Sometimes you want to see the results of a calculation in your spreadsheet without entering formula, you can do this by using the autocalculate function.

- Select the range of numbers you want to use and look at the status bar on your spreadsheet. (This is the bar at the bottom of the screen that has 'Ready' at the right hand end of it.)
- The total of the range you have selected will appear in the status bar.
- If you wish to change this to see another type of calculation, right click on this total and a menu will appear.
- Click the type of calculation you want and the answer will be calculated for you.

Check to see if your spreadsheet program has the Autocalculate function.

Autofill

Most spreadsheet programs allow you to use the Autofill facility. This is another method of reducing the time and work you do on a spreadsheet. For example, if you have a number of columns to add up, then you can use this facility.

- You highlight the cell that contains the formula you want to copy.
- Point to the bottom right hand corner of the cell – the arrow pointer will change to a black plus sign: +.
- Highlight the cells where you want to paste the formula and press enter.

Additional features

These features are more advanced but allow you to enhance the presentation of your work.

Check that your spreadsheet program can carry out the following, as some programs do not have all these facilities available.

Borders and shading

You can add different borders around your work and also shade areas of the spreadsheet as shown below.

Colour

You can also use different colours for headings etc, further enhancing your work.

	A	B	C	D	E
1	Bus fare	10.00			
2	Sweets	4.75	0.68		
3	Presents	3.99			
4	Clothes	19.89			
5	Sundries	8.00			
6	Total A	46.63			
7	Total B	26.74			
8	Total C	247.00			

Formatting

You can change the font style or size, as well as adding bold, italics, underline etc, and aligning your columns. Some of these features are shown below.

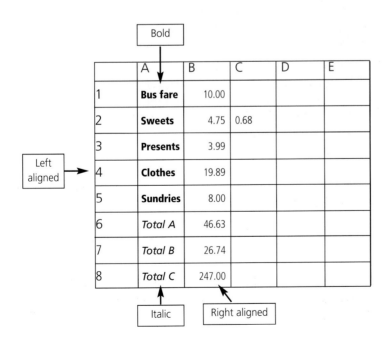

Bold

Left aligned

Italic   Right aligned

	A	B	C	D	E
1	**Bus fare**	10.00			
2	**Sweets**	4.75	0.68		
3	**Presents**	3.99			
4	**Clothes**	19.89			
5	**Sundries**	8.00			
6	*Total A*	46.63			
7	*Total B*	26.74			
8	*Total C*	247.00			

Importing

You can use the facility of importing text or graphics into your spreadsheet. You may wish to import a heading or even a logo or emblem. Some of these features are shown below.

| WordArt heading | | **Pocket Money** |

	A		B	C	D	E
1	Bus fare		10.00			
2	Sweets		4.75	0.68		
3	Presents		3.99			
4	Clothes		19.89			
5	Sundries		8.00			
6	Total A		46.63			
7	Total B		26.74			
8	Total C		247.00			

Logo → (points to row 4)

Multiple spreadsheets

You can produce many different worksheets in one spreadsheet workbook. The sheet tabs are shown at the bottom of your spreadsheet and you click on a tab to make this the active worksheet. This helps you to keep related worksheets saved in one place, thus making them easier to find.

Print preview

This allows you to see exactly what your printout will look like before you actually print it. This saves time, money and paper as you can make any necessary changes before you do the printout.

'What if'

One of the most useful functions of a spreadsheet is to set up 'what if' models. Because changing the figures in a spreadsheet causes it to recalculate automatically (if you have put the correct formulae in), it will let you see what will happen if you change the values. For example, what if the cost of a product increases by 5%?

Because a spreadsheet is a model of an actual situation, it is very useful for businesses who need to work within a budget, for example, as it allows them to alter values to do a number of 'what ifs' and find out what will happen to the total.

Let us set up a spreadsheet to see how this works.

Imagine you have been asked to make a bird table for your school grounds and you have been told that it must cost no more than £12.00. You work out what materials you need and go to the local DIY shop to find out the costs.

You put all this information into a spreadsheet.

Open a new spreadsheet and enter the following information.

BIRD TABLE PROJECT		
Materials	Amount needed	Price £
Wood for roof	2	0.74
Wood for base	2	2.16
Wood for post	1	3.75
Wood for supports	8	0.50
Nails	50	3.00
Felt for roof	1	1.25
Tacks	20	1.50
	Total	

Now put your cursor in cell C11 and click on the autosum icon. This will automatically put the formula =SUM(C4:C10) into the cell. Press enter. This should give you the total 12.90. If your total is not correct, check and change your entries.

But your budget is only £12.00 so you need to reduce your costs by £0.90. Let's try out the effect of spending only £2.75 on nails.

In cell C8 type 2.75 and press enter. The total in cell C11 reduces to 12.65.

Still too much – so try reducing the price of the roofing felt by £0.25.

In cell C9 type 1.00 and press enter. The total becomes 12.40.

Perhaps we could buy slightly cheaper wood for the post.

Type 3.30 in C6 and press enter.

There, the total is now £11.95 – within your budget! The spreadsheet has helped you by using the 'What if' function.

Save your spreadsheet, calling it 'Bird Table'. Print a copy of your spreadsheet.

Charts and graphs

Another very useful function provided by a spreadsheet is being able to change your figures into charts and graphs. This provides a visual and graphical image and makes it easier to compare numerical information.

If we go back to our Pocket Money spreadsheet, we might want to know which item had the most money spent on it each week. Of course we could just look at the figures and work it out, but it is much easier to see when we turn the information into a graph like the one below.

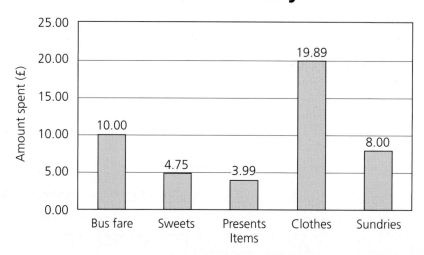

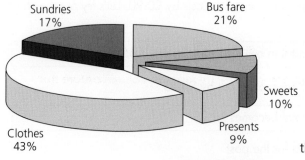

Most spreadsheet packages have many graphs and charts that you can choose from to display information and you need to practise using them and deciding which is the most appropriate one. The pie chart below shows another way of showing the same information. Which one do you think is the clearest and most effective?

Task 6.9

The way to produce graphs from spreadsheets varies depending upon the software you are using.

Find out how to create graphs on your software and produce the two graphs shown on this page.

Print out a copy of each graph.

Revision Questions

1 Spreadsheets show data in a grid of cells made up from rows and ....

lines   columns   tables   charts

2 To tell a spreadsheet what to do with the numbers you have entered, you put in
a ....

formula   message   rule   method

3 A spreadsheet can perform the mathematical functions of addition, subtraction, multiplication
and ....

taking away   division   adding   timesing

4 Spreadsheets can be used to set up .... models to test what will
happen if you change the figures.

possibility   computer   what if   maybe

5 Visual images can be produced from the figures in a spreadsheet in the form of charts
and ....

pictures   graphs   diagrams   images

6 A business can .... its sales using a spreadsheet program.

criticise   emphasise   analyse   analyse

7 Data can be entered in spreadsheets in the form of numbers, formulae
and ....

characters   words   explanations   questions

8 A spreadsheet works out calculations in a .... of the time it would
take with a calculator and pen.

double   twice   fraction   half

9 When cell referencing in a spreadsheet you always give the column before the
....

alphabet   row   space   formula

10 All formulae begin with a special ....

letter   number   character   decimal point

Task 6.10

The table below shows the number of employees in each department for 1996 and 1995.

Department	1996	1995
Sales	366	312
Service	836	738
Distribution	64	45
Administration	262	220
Totals		

1 a) Enter the above data into a spreadsheet and enter a formula for employee totals.

b) Print out a copy of the spreadsheet. Write the formula you used to calculate the employee totals on your printout. (3 marks)

2 Create a bar graph for the 1995 data. Print out a copy of the graph. (3 marks)

3 Create a pie chart comparing the number of employees in the Distribution Department in 1995 and 1996. Print out a copy of the chart. (2 marks)

4 Write a comment about the trend shown in the pie chart on the printout. (2 marks)

(Edexcel, 1997 – F and H)

Task 6.11

The file 'TPLA' contains the Trading and Profit and Loss Account for *Louisa Designs* for the financial year 1995/1996.

1 Load the file 'TPLA'.

2 Increase the width of the first column until all the labels can be seen in full and insert '£' above the two columns holding figures. (2)

3 The spreadsheet must have this heading:
Louisa Designs – Trading and Profit and Loss Account 1995/1996
Enter the heading, which **must** be left justified. (1)

4 Delete the expenses row labelled 'Extraordinary'. (1)

5 Insert a row between 'Rent/Rates' and 'Insurance' and label it 'Bank Interest'. Enter the Bank Interest figure which is £2100 in the appropriate cell. (3)

6 Net Profit is calculated by deducting Total Expenses form the Gross Profit. Using a formula enter the Net Profit into the correct cell in the third column and copy the formula you used below. (1)

7 The entries for Telephone should be £1250 and for Depreciation £2800. Make the necessary corrections. (2)

(Total 10 marks)

(Edexcel, 1996 – H)

Extension task

The following property sales have been recorded by Fuller and Brandon over the last quarter.

	October	November	December
Starter	2	4	1
Semi	7	5	3
Detached	3	3	6
Bungalow	3	4	1

The sale price for each type was:

Starter	£38,000
Semi	£65,000
Detached	£105,000
Bungalow	£33,000

1 Construct a spreadsheet, to fit on a single side of A4, which shows the monthly income and the total for the quarter from all property sales. Print out a copy of the spreadsheet.

(5 marks)

2 a) Using appropriate software, select and prepare a graph to show the monthly income from property sales for October, November and December. Print out a copy of the graph. (4 marks)

 b) Justify your choice of graph used to present this information. Write your explanation on your printout.

(3 marks)

(Edexcel, 1998 – F and H)

seven

COMMUNICATION SYSTEMS

DATABASES

At the end of this unit you should understand what:

▶ a database is

▶ a database is used for

▶ a database structure is.

You should also be able to:

▶ create a database

▶ add fields

▶ edit the database

▶ remove records

▶ sort and search

▶ create a report.

WHAT IS A DATABASE?

A database is any organised collection of data – an address book or your teacher's class register are examples of databases. We think of a database as a computerised collection of information or data.

Databases can be relatively small or they can be enormous. A small business may hold the details of all their employees in a database. For example, the Driver Vehicle Licensing Authority (DVLA) keeps data on all car owners in this country – how many records do you think they hold?

Holding this data on a computer means vast amounts of information can be stored and accessed quickly and easily. Imagine having to find information in a card-based system with a few hundred records – it would probably take you ages.

Today, data is held on each and everyone of us – sometimes without us knowing about it. Do you think your data might be held in any of the following database files:

■ your dentist

■ your doctor

■ the local library

■ your school?

Can you think of any others?

A database has many advantages over a paper-based system.

Databases	Paper-based systems
Large amounts of data can be stored on disk.	Many files would be needed to store the same amount of data.
Searching through all the records is fast.	It takes a very long time to search through all the records in all the files.
Data can be stored both alphabetically and numerically.	To file data both alphabetically and numerically, two sets of the data would need to be kept.
If back-ups are kept there is little risk of data being lost.	Some records may be lost or misplaced.
Lists/reports can be produced.	Cannot be done very easily or quickly.
Can perform calculations.	Again cannot be done easily – each record would have to be checked individually and written out manually.
Can print out address labels for mailshots.	Cannot do this.
Can be linked to a file for a mail merge	Cannot do this.

Did you think of many databases? Here are a few:

■ Stock records – a company with many different products might store details of each product using product code, price, number in stock. If there is a query, it is easy to find out whether that product is in stock or not and its location.

■ Membership details – for example, a health and fitness club will record names, addresses, telephone numbers and other personal details. Staff will be able to check when membership fees are due and what specific events members are interested in.

■ Property details for an estate agent – information about each property: the price, the number and size of rooms, whether there is a garden etc. Staff would be able to search through their records to find specific properties for clients, for example, a three-bedroomed terraced house with a large back garden.

DATABASE STRUCTURE

Files

A database **file** holds many records. All data relating to one topic is contained in one file.

The following is an example of a database file used for holding employee records.

Employee file

Records

The database file is divided into many **records**. Every record holds the same information, which, in the above example, is name, address, telephone number and department. However, the exact detail of the information is different for each record.

If a supermarket keeps information on its stock, each stock item will have its own record, containing all the details for that particular item.

If a dentist keeps patient details in a database, each patient will have their own record. What details might a dentist keep?

Fields

In each database record, there are a number of **fields**. In the employee file, the fields are employee, address, telephone number and department. In the supermarket stock file, the fields might be product code, price and whether the product is in stock or not. In the dentist's database, the fields are patient name, NHS number, address, telephone number and date of next appointment.

When setting up a database, each field will contain a specific type of information or a data type. For example, a field could contain:

- text

- number

- currency

- formula

- date

- yes/no.

What you choose will depend upon the output you want the database to give. If you want the field to make calculations it must be numeric; if you want it to show prices it must be currency with two decimal places for pence; if you always want a field to have the answer Yes or No, then the field must give a 'Yes/No' choice.

You will need to decide how much data needs to fit in each field and therefore how long each field needs to be. This means deciding on the **field length**. You need to ensure you make the field length long enough to contain all data otherwise the information will be condensed and you may not be able to read it when it is printed out.

When deciding on any numeric fields, such as currency, number and date, you need to decide on how this is to be displayed. How many decimal places do you want? Do you want a £ sign to appear? How do you want the date to look?

Good planning at this stage may save you time later on. You can, of course, alter your database in the future but try and get it right first time.

COLLECTING DATA FOR THE DATABASE

You might have collected data as part of your coursework for other subjects. How did you do this? Did you use a questionnaire? If you used a questionnaire this is called a **data capture sheet**.

There are other ways to obtain data and these are automated, for example:

- using bar codes – these appear on all goods bought in shops and supermarkets and are read by a bar code reader (See Unit 4)

- magnetic stripes – these appear on credit cards and bank cards and are swiped through a reader so that the stripe can be read. (See Unit 10)

H & E LTD

LUNCH REQUEST

To: Dining Room Manageress

Please supply the following on the date required ....

Food/drink	Number	Room	Time

Any special requirements:

Signed .... Date ....

Department ....

Using questionnaires and forms is probably the data capture method you will use most. When designing a data capture form, keep it simple and easy for the respondent to complete. As with questionnaires, do not include anything that is unnecessary.

Task 7.1

1 Try and collect as many data capture forms as you can – try local insurance companies, banks and building societies, estate agents and travel agents. If this is not possible your teacher will help you.

2 Study any forms you have collected and try and design your own data capture form.

Task 7.2

1 Details of houses for sale by Fuller and Brandon, estate agents, are kept on paper. In future these details will be kept on a database. A form for collecting information is needed, which must include:

- location of house

- price

- type

- number of bedrooms

- presence of garden/garage

- space for any other relevant details.

Use suitable software to design the form.　　(6 marks)

2 Explain TWO benefits of using a form to collect this information.　　(4 marks)

(Edexcel, 1998 – F)

EDITING THE DATABASE

Once you have created a database and saved it, you may need to edit or change it at some time in the future. This is easy to do. You may need to:

- amend a record – alter an existing record, which could be changing a telephone number

- add a new record – because a new member joins the club or a new product is offered for sale

- delete a record – remove a record because a member leaves or a house has been sold

- add new fields – because you want to add the e-mail addresses for all your members.

Task 7.3

1 You have been given the following product list for NY Fashions. Using appropriate software set up a database. Check it carefully for any errors. Give it an appropriate file name and save it.

2 Print out a copy.

Product Code	Description	Price	Size	Colour	Available
KO54	Wool trim cardigan	£56	8, 10, 12, 14, 16	Black	Y
KO55	Wool trim cardigan	£56	8, 10, 12, 14, 16	Navy	Y
OL23	Lace trim v-neck	£27	S–M, L–XL	Black	Y
OL30	Lace trim cardigan	£49	S–M, L–XL	Pink	Y
OM61	Cotton trousers	£48	8, 10, 12, 14, 16	Navy	Y
OM62	Cotton trousers – cropped	£48	8, 10, 12, 14, 16	Navy, black	Y
OM63	Cotton trousers – turn-ups	£48	8, 10, 12, 14, 16	Navy, black	Y
OW73	Velvet trim v-neck	£49	S–M, L–XL	Pink	Y
OL32	Notch neck top	£25	S–M, L–XL	Black	Y
OG18	Long printed skirt	£76	8, 10, 12, 14, 16	Multi	Y
OG26	Suede skirt	£130	8, 10, 12, 14, 16	Brown	Y
OE10	Traditional mac	£100	8, 10, 12, 14, 16	Black	Y
OE11	Traditional mac	£100	8, 10, 12, 14, 16	Navy	Y
OE12	Traditional mac	£100	8, 10, 12, 14, 16	Red	Y
OH13	Silk dress	£99	8, 10, 12, 14, 16	Multi	Y
OE15	Velvet jacket	£150	8, 10, 12, 14, 16	Black	Y
OR60	Mules	£79	36, 37, 38, 39, 40, 41	Black, navy	Y
OK38	Cropped jumper	£59	S–M, L–XL	Pink, navy	Y
OC10	Jeans	£55	8, 10, 12, 14, 16	Blue	Y
OG17	Short printed skirt	£48	8, 10, 12, 14, 16	Multi	Y
OR93	Loafers	£66	36, 37, 38, 39, 40, 41	Brown, black	Y

3 The following alterations have to be made:

■ These new products need to be added

OR21 Ankle boot £99 36, 37, 38, 39, 40, 41 Y
OM22 Suede bag £78 Y

■ The velvet jacket has been discontinued – delete this record.

■ The mules are not available at the moment.

■ The velvet trim v-neck is now £39.

4 Print out a copy of the amended database.

USING THE DATABASE

Now you have set up the database you can start to interrogate it.

Sort

This means rearranging all the records in a file into the chosen order, usually alphabetically, numerically or in date order. You can choose the order:

- from the lowest to the highest (ascending), which means from A–Z or 1–100
- from the highest to the lowest (descending), Z–A or 100–1
- in order of date.

Membership No	Surname	First Name	Address	Tel No
123	Thomas	James	34 New Road	238900
145	Ferguson	Sally	128 Brown Terrace	254228
177	Robertson	David	5 Crown Avenue	278113

Database sorted in ascending order of membership number

Membership No	Surname	First Name	Address	Tel No
145	Ferguson	Sally	128 Brown Terrace	254228
177	Robertson	David	5 Crown Avenue	278113
123	Thomas	James	34 New Road	238900

Database sorted in ascending alphabetical order of surname

Task 7.4

1 Load the database of NY Fashions and sort on the price field in ascending order.

2 Print out a copy of the database.

Search or query

If you need to find specific information you can search the database or submit a query. The NY Fashions database is not very large so it is very easy to search the records to find out any specific information. Imagine how much more difficult it would be if there were 1,000 records.

You can search **on one field** – the screen can display those products that are available.

You can search **on more than one field** at the same time – by searching on availability and price below £50.

Searching a database is done by using certain criteria. The following are symbols that can be used but you should check the software you are using:

Field name	Symbol	Definition	Example	What it means
field name	=	equal to	Description = v-neck	would find all those records with v-neck in the description
field name	< >	not equal to	Description < > trousers	would find all records that were not trousers
field name	<	less than	Price < 48	would find all records priced at less than £48
field name	>	greater than	Price > 99	would find all records priced at more than £99
field name	AND	used with another symbol	Description = mules AND size = navy	would find all records with navy mules
field name	OR	used with another symbol	Price < 48 OR > 99	would find all records priced under £48 or over £99

Searching on one field – simple search

To find out which items are priced at less than £49, you would use:

Price ⟶ less than ⟶ 49

which would give you the following list of products:

OL23	Lace trim v-neck	£27	S–M, L–XL	Black	Y
OM61	Cotton trousers	£48	8, 10, 12, 14, 16	Navy	Y
OM62	Cotton trousers – cropped	£48	8, 10, 12, 14, 16	Navy, black	Y
OM63	Cotton trousers – turn-ups	£48	8, 10, 12, 14, 16	Navy, black	Y
OW73	Velvet trim v-neck	£39	S–M, L–XL	Pink	Y
OL32	Notch neck top	£25	S–M, L–XL	Black	Y
OG17	Short printed skirt	£48	8, 10, 12, 14, 16	Multi	Y

To find out if you sell suede skirts, you would use:

description ⟶ equal to ⟶ suede skirt

which would give you the following:

OG26	Suede skirt	£130	8, 10, 12, 14, 16	Brown	Y

Searching on more than one field – complex search

If you wanted to find any items in sizes S–M, L–XL **and** in black, you would use:

size ⟶ equal to ⟶ S–M, L–XL ⟶ AND ⟶ colour ⟶ equal to ⟶ black

which would give you the following:

OL23	Lace trim v-neck	£27	S–M, L–XL	Black	Y
OL32	Notch neck top	£25	S–M, L–XL	Black	Y

Database reports

A database report means printing part or all of the information in a database. The simplest form is one that shows one whole record, which is called 'a form report'. However, you can create reports that only show information from specified fields presented in a 'table format'. For example, you might only want a copy of the Product Code and Availability fields from the NY Fashions file.

Product Code	Available
KO54	Y
KO55	Y
OL23	Y
OL30	Y
OM61	Y
OM62	Y
OM63	Y
OW73	Y
OL32	Y
OG18	Y
OG26	Y
OE10	Y
OE11	Y
OE12	Y
OH13	Y
OR60	N
OK38	Y
OC10	Y
OG17	Y
OR93	Y
OR21	Y
OM22	Y

This is what the report might look like printed out. You can also send the report to disk or display it on the screen.

For most purposes, you will use 'table reports' because they are far more effective – the information is displayed in a clear format making it suitable for quick reference. Tables also take up less paper (or fewer screens) than form reports.

Task 7.5

Load the NY Fashions file.

1 Sort the products into ascending price order.

2 Print a report to show description, size, colour and availability only.

Revision Questions

1 To keep a record of employees, Louisa Design would use a ....

fax machine   database   graphics program   accounts package

2 A collection of records in a database is called a ....

program   field   file   questionnaire

3 The secretary of the Collectors Club would make a list of all members from the database by doing what on their surnames?

sort   amend   edit   add

4 Which of these would you use a database for?

A write an application letter for a job   B store details of all your CDs
C keep the accounts of your school tuck shop   D write a notice of a forthcoming school disco

5 Which of the following would NOT be in a database of school pupils?

roll number   date of birth   marital status   registration group

Task 7.6

A video rental shop keeps a file of all videos available to rent. Some of the videos are shown below:

Video number	Video name	Type	Available	Charge – £
1905	Townscape	Thriller	Y	3.00
1912	House Sitter	Comedy	Y	3.00
1945	Funny Cartoons	Cartoon	N	2.00
1987	World War II	Adventure	Y	3.00
2865	The Hit	Thriller	N	3.00
2901	Funny Cartoons 3	Cartoon	Y	2.00

1 How many records are there in the above file?   (1 mark)

2 How many fields are there in each record?   (1 mark)

3 As new videos are bought, the shop has to amend the records. Explain what this means.   (2 marks)

4 The shop decides to sort the file in price order. Explain how this might be done.   (4 marks)

Task 7.7

Fiona Leslie has been appointed as an office manager at Louisa Designs. One of her first duties is to introduce information technology. She starts by setting up a database of all suppliers of materials to Louisa Designs. Details are in the file **SUPP**.

FIELDNAME	WIDTH	TYPE	FIELD DESCRIPTOR
CONAME	18	A	Enter company name
ADD1	25	A	Enter first line of address
ADD2	25	A	Enter second line of address
ADD3	12	A	Enter third line of address
PCODE	8	A	Enter postcode
TELNO	13	A	Enter telephone number
FAXNO	13	A	Enter fax number
MAT	8	A	Enter main material supplied
DEL	14	A	Enter method of delivery
TERMS	12	A	Enter any payment terms

1 Load the file **SUPP** and add the record below:

K Marrs & Co
112 Sevenoaks Drive
Hastings Hill
Easington
DH1 4PL
0191 5347692
0191 5499001
Lace
Courier
2.5% 7 days   (2 marks)

2 Search the database for all suppliers who supply lace. Print out a copy of these records.   (4 marks)

3 Sort the database on the postcode field and print out a copy showing company, name, address and telephone number only.   (4 marks)

(Edexcel, 1996 – F)

Extension task

Nocha Ltd uses database software to keep records of local suppliers, customers and employees.

1 Complete the diagram below by adding THREE labels from the following list:

backup   directory   field   file   record   icon

Customer name:
Customer address:
Customer postcode:
Customer telephone:
Customer fax:
Customer e-mail:

(3 marks)

2 The database directory for Nocha Ltd's local suppliers is shown below. Copy out the directory and enter the correct headings into the FOUR blank boxes below.

RECNO	3	N	Enter record number
SUPPLIER	23	A	Enter supplier business name
CONTACT	20	A	Enter contact name, surname, initial
CTEL	8	A	Enter contact telephone number
FITEM	20	A	Enter food item supplier

(3 marks)

3 Nocha Ltd's database of its suppliers is called SUPPLY.

a) Load SUPPLY. (Your teacher will have keyed this data in for you.) Add to the database a new supplier from the details given below.

Peerless Ltd is a supplier of flavouring. The contact is Sylvia Woodward and her telephone number is 762238.   (2 marks)

b) Find the supplier ADMF and change the food item to citric acid.   (1 mark)

c) Delete the supplier Radnot Essence.   (1 mark)

d) Print out a copy of the database showing all fields.   (1 mark)

e) Sort the database on the SUPPLIER field and print out a copy of the database, showing supplier, contact and telephone number only.   (2 marks)

f) Search the database for the companies that supply flavourings. Print out a copy of the database, showing the supplier field only.   (1 mark)

(Edexcel, 1999 – F)

Task 7.8

Docdel plc keeps records of employees and their cars on a database. A database directory of employees at Docdel plc is shown below. Complete the blank spaces in the TYPE column.

FIELD	WIDTH	TYPE	FIELD DESCRIPTOR
RECNO	5		Record number
NAME	20		Surname then first initial
POSIT	20		Position within Docdel
DEPT	15		Department they work in
REGY	4		Year of car's first registration
REGN	10		Registration number
MAKE	12		Make of car
ABM	6		Agreed business mileage
LITRE	4		Engine capacity

Load the file EMP (your teacher will have keyed in this data for you).

a) David Turner, a new salesperson, has just received his car. The details are given below. Add his record to the file EMP.

   1.4 Fiat, registration N643 NGE, first registered in 1996, agreed business mileage will be 15,000.

   Print out a copy of this record.   (2 marks)

b) The Finance Director has just taken delivery of his new car. It is a 1996 registered Jaguar, N232 DDE, with a 5.2 litre engine. Make amendments as necessary to his record. Print out a copy of the amended record.
                                                    (2 marks)

c) Sort the file EMP on the REGY and MAKE fields. Include all fields. Print out.   (2 marks)

(Edexcel, 1997 – H)

Task 7.9

The Ice Cream Alliance keeps a database of its members. It needs updating.

1 Load the file **MEMBERS** (your teacher may have keyed in this data for you).

a) Guidis has gone out of business. Delete this record.

(1 mark)

b) The following have recently joined The Ice Cream Alliance. Add their details.

Dominos, Middleton Grange, Winchester, RO4 3RG, Tel: 01823 866531 Fax: 01823 908758, Wholesale

Stans, Dene View, Winchester, RO2 4BR, Tel: 01823 976542 Fax: 01823 966711, Retail

Print out a copy of the database. (2 marks)

c) Search the database for those members who offer both retail and wholesale services. Sort alphabetically on the name field. Include only SUPPLIER, TEL and TYPE fields. (2 marks)

2 Explain why The Ice Cream Alliance uses a database instead of keeping paper records. (4 marks)

(Edexcel, 1999 – H)

eight

COMMUNICATION SYSTEMS

DESKTOP PUBLISHING

At the end of this unit you should understand what:

▶ desktop publishing is

▶ desktop publishing is used for.

You should also be able to use desktop publishing software to:

▶ integrate text and graphics

▶ import files from different sources

▶ use templates and style sheets

▶ crop images

▶ produce overhead transparencies, which can be used in presentations.

WHAT IS DESKTOP PUBLISHING?

Desktop publishing (DTP) software will allow you to produce documents where you have combined pictures and text. You can arrange the text into columns with headlines. Pictures or images can be imported from clip art or you can scan images as you want to.

DTP lets you do the same job as you would with word processing but you can be more particular about the presentation of your document with regard to where you place your text and pictures on the page.

The documents that you can produce with DTP can be pages for a newsletter or magazine, advertisements, leaflets, menus, price lists and transparencies for presentations on the overhead projector.

Advantages of desktop publishing

1 High-quality documents can be produced quickly, especially if a laser printer is used.

2 Production costs will be lower than using an external printing firm, which could be expensive.

3 All documents used in the company will be improved, which will enhance the image of the company.

4 Layouts can be changed and amendments made easily because everything is saved.

Desktop publishing facilities

Text

You can prepare your text on the word processor, save it and then load it into the DTP. It is then possible to change and alter the text as you want to. You can type the text straight into DTP but the editing facilities are not as good in DTP, so for large amounts of text it is better to word-process it first.

You can also import text from other files, for example, you may have something you have received through e-mail and wish to insert it into your new document.

Fonts

You have many different font or text types to choose from. A few examples are:

Advert

Arial Narrow

Century Schoolbook

Courier

Geneva

Sabon

Times

In fact, having a wide selection of fonts is one of the key features in DTP.

While the same fonts may be available in the word processor, you cannot manipulate them as you can with DTP. You can change the font size and position, as well as scale them in DTP. This means you can vary the size of the font but still retain the correct shape of the characters.

As well as changing the size of the font, you can change the space between the characters and also change the space between one line and the next, which is what helps give DTP documents their professional look.

Here are a few different font sizes to give you some idea of what they look like:

8 point

10 point

12 point

14 point

16 point

18 point

38 point

48 point

Images

Pictures can be included in DTP, which is a very important facility. These may be diagrams, scanned images, drawings and anything from the clip art library. You can also use a graphics library, which includes symbols, such as arrows, and symbols used in architectural or technical drawings.

You can use symbols and logos created by others and saved on disk, for example, you can use your school badge in any school publications. Your school may have this already saved in a file.

Here are examples of some symbols you can use.

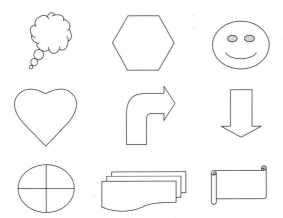

Special effects

Special effects are available for text. These are intended to add to the appearance but, as with all special effects, they should be used with care. Too many and your documents will look messy. You should be able to:

- change the angle of the text by rotating it

- vary the angle of individual characters

- crop an image – this means to cut off part of an image

- insert a fancy initial capital at the beginning of a line.

Drawing

The DTP software will include some drawing facilities. However, as with typing in text, it is sometimes easier to create any drawings with graphics software and import them into documents later.

Page layout

In order to produce an attractive document, it is essential that you plan the page layout carefully. If column layout is required this should be specified when the page layout is created, as should the space between the columns and the widths of the columns.

Any images, symbols, graphics and blocks of text can be moved around, resized or edited.

The layering facility can be used. This means the ability to position pictures over text or position text over pictures. In order to get a layering effect, you will need to select the object and 'Send to Back' or 'Bring to Front'.

It is also possible to make the text background transparent so that the picture or image can be seen behind the text. This is a very effective facility, which you should experiment with.

Task 8.1

Your headteacher would like you to design new headed paper for your school. Try and get hold of a copy of the existing paper. What about trying to use your school logo?

Consistency

Most companies like the style of their published material – letterheads, memoranda and reports – to be consistent and in keeping with their corporate image. They will probably have a basic design or document style that is used frequently. This design is called a **template** or **style sheet** and once it has been designed it can be saved and then retrieved at any time. This means it is not necessary to design each document from scratch every time, which saves a lot of time and effort.

The template or style sheet provides a framework into which text and data can be added. It makes it possible to specify particular styles of text font and size, as well as the layout of the page – whether lines are centred, indented or fully blocked – and use of colour, background, borders and shading etc.

Because these styles are saved they can be retrieved and applied to any section of the document. You would need to highlight the particular text, eg a paragraph, then select the paragraph style from the menu list.

The advantages of using templates or style sheets are:

- it is quick and easy to apply formatting to highlighted text throughout the document
- it is easy to be consistent when working with long documents – it ensures the same style is used throughout the document
- it ensures a house style is used in all documentation.

Design

It is not difficult to create a document using DTP – here are some simple rules to help you when designing:

- look at existing page and document designs to get some ideas
- remember who your audience is and use a suitable design
- remember what the purpose of the document is
- keep the design simple – do not use too many fonts and sizes
- be consistent – do not keep changing styles
- draw a draft on paper first
- remember the use of white space, which we discussed in Unit 2 – use it effectively.

PRESENTATIONS

In business, it is important that information is accurate, up to date and relevant. All these are possible using the business communication systems that we have looked at up to now. All systems combine to produce material that is of a high quality, which contributes to the corporate image of the company and how people view the company.

The presentation quality available through DTP has transformed how a business presents itself to others. Businesses need to make visual presentations and these can be produced easily with DTP. These presentations use a combination of different types of information, which we know may include text, charts and diagrams. The presentation is a means of giving information to an audience. Whether this is a few people or many, the aims are the same – to get over the information in as clear and interesting a way as possible.

However, the use of specific presentation software, like PowerPoint, can be used to prepare overhead transparencies consisting of text, charts, diagrams and pictures to add to the effectiveness of any presentation. It is possible to link a PC to an overhead projector screen so that information can be seen by everyone at the meeting.

PowerPoint allows us to prepare slides, which can be linked together to make up a complete presentation. The different types of slides are as follows.

Text slides

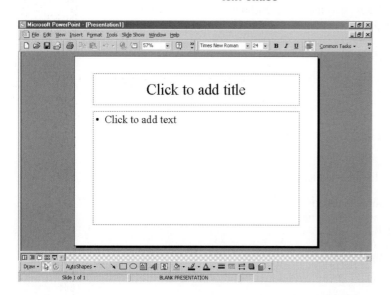

These slides consist of brief points, which are sometimes bulleted or preceded with an asterisk. A good bit of advice is not to include too much information on each slide – five pieces of information is considered ideal, otherwise the audience will lose interest if there is too much to read and take in.

Tables, chart or graph slides

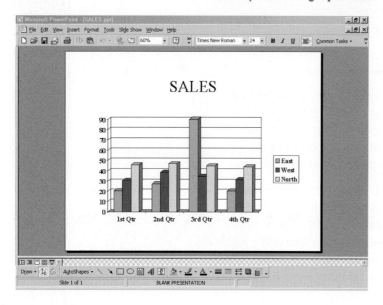

As with the text slides, the table, chart or graph must not be too complicated. The reason for its inclusion in the presentation is to simplify lots of figures – the aim is not to confuse the audience.

Diagram or flow chart slides

Being able to project a diagram or flow chart onto a screen, which everyone can see and which can be explained, makes a very effective way of presenting something that might otherwise have proved complicated.

The PowerPoint screen above shows how easy it is to create a slide containing an organisation chart. All you need to do is add your own information and details.

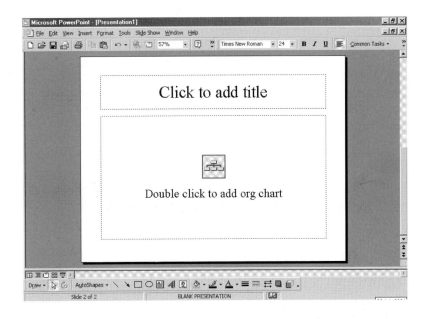

Photos or clip art slides

Digitised photographs can be used, as well as any clip art available to you.

When all slides are created the whole presentation can be linked together. The software will let you choose the slides to be included and you can then decide the order in which they will be presented.

The software will let you decide how long you want each slide to remain on the screen. You can also choose how you want each slide to appear on the screen or disappear from the screen – do you want the slides to fade out or scroll up from the bottom? You can even add sound effects.

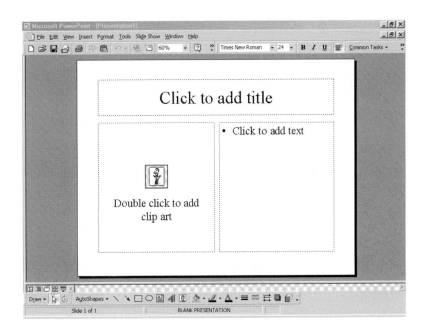

Task 8.2

You designed the headed paper for your school earlier, now try and design the front cover of your school prospectus.

Remember, keep it simple and do not forget who your audience is.

Task 8.3

Fuller and Brandon are estate agents and produce house details for their clients. Using appropriate DTP software, prepare an A4 notice from the following notes and instructions.

Prepare a sheet for prospective buyers for the detached houses on 'Sleepy Hollow' – details are:

5 bedrooms, 2 en-suite, bathroom and downstairs cloakroom. Power points in all rooms except bathroom and downstairs cloakroom (shaver socket in bathroom and en-suite) double garage and parking for 3 cars. Entrance to garage via utility room. All ceilings artex and coving. Gas central heating. Kitchen and utility room. Separate dining room. Utility room plumbed for washing machine. All windows sealed double glazing. Front garden open plan and back garden patio and lawn.

TV sockets in lounge, dining room and 2 bedrooms. Kitchen, bathroom, cloakroom tiled to client choice. Spacious entrance hall, upstairs landing.

NB. Leave space for artist's impression and site plan. Do not forget to include the price. (10 marks)

(Edexcel, 1998 – H)

Task 8.4

New computers and software mean that Happy Ideas Ltd can now produce its own advertising material.

Using appropriate DTP software, prepare an advertisement for the New Millennium Bear. Include any of the information below that you think is necessary.   (6 marks)

ADDRESS: 2 FACTORY LANE, STONEYBRIDGE SB4 7BR

AVAILABLE
FROM MARCH
2000

CAN BE ORDERED FROM
MANY BEAR SHOPS

TEL 01952 339741
EMAIL HL@AOL.COM

GRAPHIC
COULD BE
INCLUDED

(Edexcel, 2000 – F)

Maggie and Charles, the owners of Teddies on the Circle have decided to produce an A4 leaflet for customers to pick up when they come to the shop. Charles has made a note of some ideas. His notes are shown below.

GRAPHIC OF A BEAR AT TOP

NAME OF SHOP – EMPHASISED AND CENTRED

A4 LEAFLET IDEAS!

STONEYBRIDGE – IMPORTANT HISTORICAL SITE

LARGE SHOP, 1000 OF BEARS, 70 MAKERS

OPEN DAILY 10–6

TELEPHONE 01952 334942

NEW E-MAIL ADDRESS TEDDIES@aol.com
NB ADDRESS/ TEL NO AND E-MAIL AT BOTTOM – ADDRESS FIRST

BULLETS
THINGS WE OFFER!
MAIL ORDER
CREDIT CARDS – ALL
CLUB STORE FOR HAPPY IDEAS LTD
TEDDY GIFTS
DEPOSIT ON A BEAR SECURES

ADDRESS
3 THE CRESCENT STONEYBRIDGE SB4 9JR

1   Use appropriate DTP software and the above notes to design a leaflet.   (5 marks)

2   Describe how you used the facilities in your chosen software to design and produce the leaflet.   (6 marks)

(Edexcel, 2000 – H)

nine

COMMUNICATION SYSTEMS

PEOPLE

At the end of this unit you should understand:

▸ the different methods of communication between people through:

  ▸ informal and formal meetings

  ▸ groups

  ▸ discussions

  ▸ presentations

  ▸ interviews

  ▸ face-to-face communication

how these different methods of communication are used in different business situations.

MEETINGS

A meeting is a gathering of people for a particular purpose and a vital communication channel for business. A **public meeting** is one that is open to all who wish to attend. This kind of meeting is often held to discuss a matter of general concern, such as a proposal to site a mobile phone mast near a local primary school.

A **private meeting** is different. The general public is not invited and attendance is restricted to those entitled to be there.

In a business, meetings will be organised to communicate and discuss company policy. The meetings may be internal departmental meetings, meetings of the board of directors or general meetings of the shareholders. Each of these meetings will have different business to discuss but will probably follow the basic format which you learnt about in Unit 2.

Departmental or other internal meetings are usually **informal** and a written record of what took place may not always be made, although sometimes minutes may be kept. For example, if a year head had a meeting with form representatives, no record would be kept.

However, major meetings, such as the Annual General Meeting of a business, will be **formal** and an agenda will be followed and minutes kept of what takes place or what is decided at the meeting.

Effective meetings

Good meetings do not just happen – they take careful planning. Otherwise, people think they are a waste of time, which can cause frustration. The following is a checklist that will help to ensure meetings are events where genuine communication occurs.

- Everyone attending the meeting is clear about why they are there and what they want out of the meeting.

- The objectives of the meeting, as far as possible, are achieved.

- There is enough time to discuss everything on the agenda.

- The agenda is followed and no time is wasted with unnecessary discussion.

- Everyone at the meeting is allowed to have their say.

- Decisions and appropriate action is agreed.

- The appropriate action is put into practice.

Task 9.1

1 Explain what a meeting is.

2 What is the difference between a formal and an informal meeting?

3 State THREE examples of formal meetings. (10 marks)

GROUPS

As well as formal and informal meetings, we have formal and informal groups in business, as you learnt in Unit 1. **Formal groups** in business are set up to carry out specific tasks. These could be departments – Personnel or Production – or groups could be set up from time to time to tackle particular projects, for example, how the introduction of a new computer network could be handled.

An **informal group** is not set up by the business but it comes into existence itself. As you learnt earlier, examples of these groups might be friends who play football together after work or who enjoy taking part in pub quizzes.

Managers think that businesses seem to perform best when employees act not as individuals but as members of highly efficient work groups, because of this, groups are now formed and encouraged within most businesses.

People want to feel accepted as part of a group. A business that encourages employees to feel part of a team or group, will probably have very low rates of absenteeism and high levels of motivation. A well-motivated workforce is more likely to work hard, which should see the business do well through keeping costs down, increasing profits and being competitive.

Team building and ice-breaking

In order for formal groups to operate effectively there are strategies used to help the group establish itself, so the members of the group get on with each other and work well together.

These strategies are designed so that the group gets to know each other and they help take away the feeling of tension or awkwardness in a new group. If the group have been together some time or have worked together before, there is much less need for this kind of activity. Something as simple as learning each other's names and job roles would be a start as this actively involves everyone.

An activity that is considered an ice-breaker might be each member of the group volunteering in turn to speak about something that happened to them in the week. It is up to the individual to choose the topic and, as the activity progresses, other team members are encouraged to make comments and ask questions. By sharing experiences with others empathy develops and this is the first step towards the group becoming a supportive unit. If the group is able to build up a good rapport, this will make work done later considerably easier, as much of what the group will be required to do will probably involve group interdependence.

One thing that should be avoided is for cliques to develop, so learning how to work using co-operational and negotiating skills is important. An activity like 'What to throw out of the lifeboat' is good for this. Group members have to reach a consensus on what to throw out of the lifeboat otherwise it will sink. In order to do this, they have to discuss, appraise, negotiate and persuade, which helps establish relationships, develop group rapport and enables the personal qualities of individuals to become evident, such as natural leadership or good negotiation skills.

DISCUSSIONS

Talking is probably the way we communicate most of all. What you say and how you say it depends on:

- who you are speaking to

- the reason for speaking to that person

- where this discussion takes place.

If you are speaking to someone you know and you are discussing a topic that you are familiar with, then you are probably not anxious, because you are in control and you do not feel threatened. Unfortunately, this is not always the case, as there will be times when you are required to discuss things with strangers and, for some of us, this can prove stressful. Being able to cope in these situations because you have good oral skills is very useful and employers value it enormously. Imagine having to deal with an angry customer!

Being in a discussion calls for certain basic skills:

- Try to be clear in what you say – do not use more words than you need to or words that others may not understand.

- Adopt a suitable tone for the people you are talking to – do not sound too patronising.

- Listen carefully to others involved – respect the views of others and their right to speak also.

- Ask suitable questions that will help your understanding of the issues, if you need to.

- Do not assume that others in the discussion understand everything or alternatively that they understand nothing.

- Do your homework beforehand so you know as much as you can about the subject of the discussion; then you will be well prepared.

Task 9.2

1 Read the following statements and write beside each one whether you think it would help or hinder a discussion.

- Not listening to others
- Repeating the same point
- Moving things on
- Putting others down
- Making suggestions
- Seeking the ideas and opinions of others
- Taking over the discussion
- Giving support to others' ideas
- Calming down trouble
- Thinking aloud
- Resolving conflict
- Being honest and open
- Showing disagreement
- Summarising what others have said
- Criticising others
- Talking over people

Add any others you can think of.

2 In a discussion, you have to talk about a topic of particular interest to you. Choose a topic you could talk about and prepare a list or spidergram of what you think you should include.

PRESENTATIONS

There may be times when you will be required to stand up in front of a group of people and to talk to them. There will be many reasons you need to talk to a group of people and you may feel nervous. The better prepared you are the more successful you will be and the happier you will be to do a presentation in the future.

Before the presentation

Know how long the presentation is expected to last. People start to lose concentration after about thirty minutes so, if you have not been given a definite time, try to keep it to less than thirty minutes.

Prepare yourself by arriving early to look at the room. Make sure there are plenty of seats. Check there is an overhead projector if you need one – and that it works!

Look neat and tidy and have your notes and visual aids ready and in order.

Making a presentation

Know the subject matter really well in case someone asks you a specific question. If you are having difficulty in answering a question, you may have to admit you do not know the answer but that you will find out.

Know exactly what you are going to say. You may need to write down every word until you feel sufficiently relaxed not to have to refer to the notes but you will still have them as a back-up if you need them. Some presenters use key words jotted down on small cards instead of using sheets and sheets of paper. These are sometimes known as cue cards.

Make sure you do not speak too quietly or too quickly – this is one way of losing the attention of your audience.

You may want to use charts and diagrams to illustrate points, which will help the audience understand the more technical or complicated parts of your presentation. It will also break up the presentation so your audience does not become bored.

Smile at the audience and try to look confident even if you do not feel it! There will be sympathetic people in the audience who will be on your side – if there is someone who smiles or nods at you then it would appear they like what you are saying – a good sign.

Introduce yourself and outline the subject of the presentation. Always try to keep it simple. Do not use complicated words or jargon; use short words and sentences.

Make eye contact with the audience – there is nothing worse than a speaker looking up to the ceiling or finding something really interesting to look at on the floor!

Remember your body language. Do you have any irritating mannerisms? Ask a friend if he or she thinks you have, then try to put them right.

Finally do not panic if you forget something or dry up. Pausing in a presentation gives the audience a break and gives you the opportunity to check your notes or take a breath. Chances are that someone will use the break to ask a question or make a comment.

Remember, if you are well prepared and well organised, the successful delivery will follow – be enthusiastic and enjoy the experience. It gets easier every time!

Task 9.3

1 You have to research and prepare a short talk – to last no more than TWO minutes. It can be on any topic of interest to you but discuss this with your teacher.

2 Each person in the group will deliver their talk while the rest of the class uses the feedback sheet below to assess each speaker.

3 After each person has delivered their talk, discuss with your teacher what you thought the good and bad points were.

Name of presenter.................... Topic ....

Appearance

Neat and tidy	1	2	3	4	5
Body language	1	2	3	4	5
Eye contact	1	2	3	4	5
Nervous/enthusiastic	1	2	3	4	5

Presentation

Was there an introduction?	1	2	3	4	5
Was the presentation organised?	1	2	3	4	5
Was it easy to follow?	1	2	3	4	5
Were questions well handled?	1	2	3	4	5

1 = low, 5 = high

INTERVIEWS

There are many types of interview but the one you will be most concerned about is the job interview.

Applications will be received for jobs, these are considered and a selection made of those who seem most suitable for the job. These applicants are called 'the shortlist' and are invited for an interview.

The interview helps an employer assess these selected applicants and to arrive at a decision on their suitability for the job. It also gives the applicants an opportunity of seeing the premises and asking questions about the job.

No matter how confident you are, you are not likely to look forward to an interview – not many of us do. The key to a successful interview is, as we have just learnt with presentations and meetings, to plan and prepare thoroughly.

Before the interview

1 You might want to find out some information about the organisation where the job is. Some knowledge of the history of the company might be useful.

2 Plan your journey – make sure you know how to get to the interview. Check the times of buses and trains and leave plenty of time to allow for delays. If you can, make a dummy run first – it doesn't look good arriving flustered and in a panic – punctuality is important.

3 You should appear clean, tidy and smartly dressed. Plan what you are going to wear in advance. Try it on beforehand – does it need dry cleaning, are there any buttons missing, does it still fit? Choose an appropriate outfit for the job – leather jackets and jeans will not be appropriate for many jobs! First impressions are important and at interviews these tend to be formed when the candidate enters the room.

4 You might be good at off-the-cuff comments and remarks at school but, in an interview situation, you might dry up on the day, so prepare a few notes on why you want the job and why you think you are suitable. Jot down some questions to ask, such as does the company offer training and are there opportunities for promotion? You want little to worry about on the day so this preparation will help.

5 Try not to panic – everyone suffers from nerves but you need to learn how to cope with your nerves so you do not go to pieces. Deep breaths help, as does keeping your hands in your lap – try to think positive and remember that most interviewers are trained to assess your personality and ability and can see through nerves.

During the interview

6 As stated earlier, first impressions are important, so try to be confident as you walk into the room. Make eye contact with the interviewer and smile. If he or she offers to shake your hand, do so with a firm, not bone crushing, handshake.

7 Sit firmly on the chair – do not perch on the edge otherwise you will never be able to relax.

8 Remember everything that has been said about body language. One of the advantages of talking to people rather than writing to them is that you can immediately see their reactions but remember that this is two-way. The interviewer is forming an impression of how you are reacting just as you can see how the interviewer is reacting to what you say. Shrugging the shoulders, looking out of the window or at your watch will not create a very good impression. Remember to think about how you look as well as what you are saying.

9 Try to speak clearly and appear as natural as you can. Answers to questions should be relevant and as knowledgeable as possible. Try to avoid 'yes' or 'no' answers – the interviewer is trying to find out whether or not you could do the job so try to help yourself by answering sensibly. If you do not know the answer to a question it is best to say so. Interviewers appreciate an honest approach.

FACE TO FACE

When dealing with people in an organisation there are many occasions when it is necessary to talk face to face with them. They might be people you know and work with or people you do not know, or even visitors. They might be people who already have some knowledge of the topic under discussion or they may have no previous knowledge at all. It might be that you are required to talk to someone at a higher level than you in the company. Whatever the situation, you will be expected to have the skills and confidence to cope.

It will be your job to give a good impression of both you and the company. At first you may feel very shy and nervous because you are frightened of making a mistake or making a fool of yourself. But remember that strangers or visitors might also feel nervous – a friendly smile together with a pleasant greeting can make a difference to the way a meeting goes.

Verbal communication skills

In any form of face-to-face communication having good verbal communication skills is important. Not being able to make yourself understood or getting tongue-tied can be a handicap but with practice it is quite easy to improve.

Sometimes verbal communication is more appropriate than written communication so it is important to remember that verbal communication:

- is direct and quick

- can be more informal than other forms of communication

- can be used to inform, persuade, instruct and demand

- can be very persuasive

- can provide instant feedback.

Always think about what you are saying and try to give accurate and clear information. It is easy to write and rewrite but once said the spoken word cannot be taken back – so try to avoid saying anything that is unclear or incomplete and therefore confusing.

Be prepared to listen to the other person. There is nothing more irritating than someone always butting in and interrupting (even if you are bored!) – it disturbs the thought processes and can sometime take the speaker longer to get to the point. You have two ears and one mouth – try to use them in that proportion!

Have you heard the expression 'it's not what you say but the way that you say it ...'? Imagine you are asking a favour of someone – unless you adopt the right tone it is unlikely that the favour will be granted. Would it be better to ask the favour in a pleasant tone or in an abrupt, rude tone?

No matter what the circumstances, adopting an aggressive or bullying tone almost never works. You have to remember who you are speaking to and adopt the most suitable tone. What tone of voice would you use with your boss who wanted some information urgently or how would you speak to a nervous new colleague?

THE CUSTOMER/CLIENT RELATIONSHIP

The ability to communicate is probably the most important function of any organisation. Communication is the process by which planning, organising, leading, directing and controlling are accomplished. Good communication is essential to present a positive image of the organisation as it links the organisation with customers/clients and the wider community. It should reduce conflict and prevent unnecessary misunderstanding.

Externally, it is important that customers and callers are treated courteously and dealt with appropriately. All responses to customers and clients should be effective so relations remain positive and friendly. A rapport needs to be built up between customers and clients.

Internally, liaison and communication between individuals and departments should also be effective. Everyone in the organisation needs to be sure of their job role in their functional area. Poor communication results in mistakes being made, anxiety for employees and customers, the low morale of employees and can lead to the loss of customers.

It is vital that effective channels and systems of communication are used as these contribute to the success of the organisation. A variety of systems should be used and the organisation should ensure that the monitoring and improvement of systems is a continual process. In addition, all employees must be aware of the importance of good communication and be encouraged to play their part in developing and improving communication systems in the organisation thereby ensuring no communication failures.

Revision Questions

1 A shortlist of job applicants consists of those

   A   who nearly got the job

   B   who are to be invited for an interview

   C   who can begin work at short notice

   D   who sent a letter that was too short

2 Which of the following is not the purpose of a job interview?

   A   to test the candidate's intelligence

   B   to give the candidate the opportunity to ask questions

   C   to assess the candidate's appearance

   D   to assess the candidate's suitability for the job

3 It is sensible to make a .... of a job application letter before writing it out in detail.

   rough draft   carbon copy   photocopy   fax

4 A job .... is where an employer assesses the suitability of an applicant for employment.

   interview   reference   description   specification

5 An interview gives the job applicant the opportunity to demonstrate their ability to
   ....

   write   communicate   listen   discuss

6 Managers of Harbon Estates Ltd hold regular meetings at their offices. This form of communication is

   e-mail   face to face   written   vertical

7 People wanting seasonal employment at Nocha Ltd have to complete .... before they are interviewed.

   a letter   a contract   an application form   a payslip

8 When Nina Klaus has a face-to-face meeting with Julia Clements, she communicates by ....

   speaking   reading   information technology writing

9 Explain the difference between formal and informal meetings.

10 Why might a business want feedback in the communication process?

Task 9.4

All applicants for positions at Docdel plc must complete an application form. Select from the list below three items that would be included in an application form. Explain why each one is on the form.

| referees | hours worked | qualification |
| wages | job title | duties |

(6 marks)

(Edexcel, 1997 – F)

Task 9.5

Nocha Ltd has a rush order for ginger ice cream. Gino Nocha arranges an immediate meeting with the Office Manager, Laura Hughes.

Explain why Gino has a meeting with Laura Hughes rather than using the telephone. (4 marks)

(Edexcel, 1999 – F and H)

Task 9.6

Analyse each of the following media for communication.

a) formal meeting
b) presentation
c) interview

(12 marks)

Extension task

Communication is an important aspect of management. Two-way communication, with some feedback, is more useful than one-way. Do you agree with this statement? Give your reasons.

(12 marks)

DATA GATHERING, RECORDING AND PRESENTATION SYSTEMS

DATA GATHERING AND STORAGE

At the end of this unit you should be able to understand:

▸ how data is gathered manually

▸ how data is stored manually

▸ how data is captured and stored electronically.

METHODS OF COLLECTING DATA MANUALLY

Organisations gather data manually from different sources using a variety of methods, for example, surveys where data is collected directly from a sample of the population using questionnaires and interviews.

One of the most common ways to gather data manually is by questionnaire. An example of a questionnaire is the Census which took place in April 2001. Every household in the UK received a census which required the completion of questions about each person living at that address. The forms were either returned to the Census Office by post or collected by a census official.

Some organisations collect data by post. An example of this might be when someone buys a new car. After a couple of months they may be sent a questionnaire through the post to ask them if they are satisfied with the car and the garage that sold it to them. The company will hope that the customer will send the questionnaire back so that they can see what kind of things please customers and what displeases them.

A different method of collecting data is by interviews. Interviewers are employed to stop people in the street and ask them questions. For example, they may ask about the type of chocolate bar you prefer and how often you buy it. The person asking the questions will often fill in the questionnaire as you answer because this saves time. Interviews are also carried out over the telephone, with the interviewer completing the questionnaire during the conversation.

STORING DATA MANUALLY

Once data has been collected it needs to be processed and stored. We will look at the main methods that are used to store data manually. Data is usually 'filed' – this means storing it in some kind of order so that it can be found easily by anyone who needs to have access to it. Filing can be done alphabetically, numerically, chronologically etc. Each organisation will decide for itself which is the most logical way to file its paper-based data.

Alphabetical filing

This is filing using the alphabet from A to Z. In most cases data is filed using names, but sometimes it could be addresses or departments. For example, most doctors file patients' records in alphabetical order using their last name.

In this example, the following names need to be filed alphabetically:

Jones
Smith
Baker
Woolley

If they were filed in the correct alphabetical order, they would appear like this:

Baker
Jones
Smith
Woolley

Numerical filing

This is filing using numbers. One example of this would be a company roll number. Each employee is given a roll number when he/she starts to work for the company and they keep this number throughout their service. This is done because there could be several employees with the same name, but each will have a unique roll number. This helps to prevent confusion. Record cards showing details about each of the employees would be filed in roll number order starting with the lowest number. This system makes it easy to find the record card for any employee.

An example of numerical filing would be:

11678
11987
12402
15023

Here the numbers start with the lowest and get higher.

Chronological filing

This is a method of filing in date order and is often used to file business documents such as copies of invoices and statements. These are filed in order of the dates that they are sent out to customers.

For example, if we were filing the following dates in chronological order:

20/04/2001
17 April 1954
18 March 1985
25 June 1999

They would read as follows:

17 April 1954
18 March 1985
25 June 1999
20/4/2001

The oldest date is placed first with the more recent date at the end.

Filing, or putting records away is often regarded as a dull and rather unimportant job, but if an organisation is to operate efficiently using paper-based records, it is important that filing is done very carefully. Once a record has been filed out of sequence, it is extremely difficult to find again.

Paper-based filing systems have been replaced in most organisations by electronic systems which are much quicker to access and amend, but many companies still have a paper system as a back-up in case their computers crash meaning they do not have access to their computer records.

Collating

It is sometimes necessary to collate data that has been gathered so that it is presented in a more useful format. Two examples of this might be:

- when you have found out the advantages and disadvantages of a particular system, you put them into the form of a table to make them easier to read.

- a form tutor might gather together all the subject reports for the pupils in their form group and collate them into the correct sequence to make up each pupil's yearly report.

Revision control

All data has to be revised and kept up-to-date. This may be as simple as finding a record that has been filed and updating it with new details; for example, a new address would need to be updated on an employee's record card.

However, sometimes a revision is more formal. For example when a textbook is written, after a period of time it may go out of date and a new version will be produced. The author will delete information that is no longer relevant and perhaps include new chapters. This is called a revised edition and the front page of the book will tell you which edition you are looking at and the date when it was published.

Another example of formal revision control is when the specifications for an examination are being prepared. A draft copy will be written first and before this is accepted as the final copy it will have to go through various stages of approval. This might mean that changes have to be made and a number of new versions of the original document will be produced. Each version will have the revision details on it, usually consisting of the title of the document and the date of revision. This generally appears at the bottom of each page of the document so that all the people concerned are clear which version they are looking at. The revision details could read like this:

Draft Specification Edexcel GCSE Business and Communication Systems (revised September 2000).

The date would change with each new version.

HOW DATA IS CAPTURED ELECTRONICALLY

To study electronic data capture, we need to look at methods of capturing data and entering it into a computer. The system used will depend upon where the data is coming from. We will look at a number of different methods and why various organisations might use them.

Keyboards

Most text-based data that is entered into a computer is input via a keyboard. The data is often copied from a paper document, for example, an application form for a job or to open a bank account or an enrolment form for a sports club.

Often large amounts of data have to be entered, and it is common nowadays to use a batch processing system. Data is input using a keyboard and stored immediately on disk. The data is not processed until it is needed, when it is downloaded from the disk onto the main computer ready for use.

Advantages of keyboard data entry:

- It requires little expertise.

- It is relatively inexpensive because it uses existing software packages.

- It does not require specialist stationery and equipment.

Disadvantages of keyboard data entry:

- It is time consuming because a great deal of data is processed twice.

- Errors are often made because of difficulty interpreting data to be processed, eg handwriting.

- The work is often mundane.

The rest of the methods of data entry that we shall look at in this section are automated, which means that data is read directly into the computer electronically.

Optical mark reader (OMR)

An optical mark reader enters data directly from a document into a computer rather than using a keyboard. The reader detects marks, which have been made in exactly the right places on a form or document and reads the data into the memory of the computer. The specially designed forms or documents have empty boxes to put the marks in using a pencil.

Examples of the use of this method are multiple-choice examination papers, market research questionnaires and school registers. One of the main advantages of the system is that data can be entered without using any special equipment, as soon as it is collected. For example, a class register is marked at registration time and the data for the whole school can be entered into the computer via the reader within ten minutes of the end of registration.

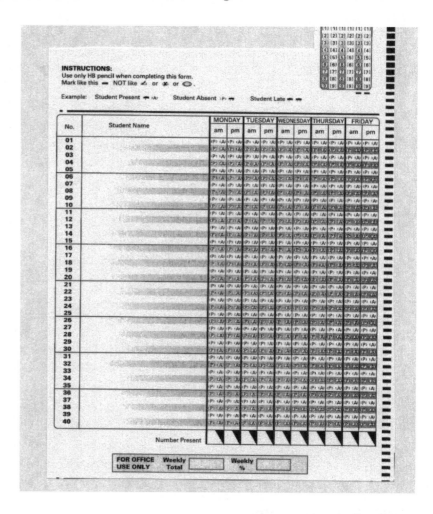

Advantages of optical mark reading:

■ It is fast – large amounts of data can be processed rapidly.

■ There is less chance of errors because of pre-set answers.

Disadvantages of optical mark reading:

■ The scanners are very expensive – starting at around £5000.

■ It requires pre-printed stationery.

■ It requires great accuracy on the part of the user.

■ It is a relatively expensive method because it requires teamwork between the organisation using the forms and the suppliers who design the forms.

Task 10.1

1 Think back to when you took your SATS tests in year 9. Why do you think it was important that you put the marks that represented your answers on the OMR answer sheet in exactly the right places?

2 What could you have done to change a mark that was put in the wrong place?

Optical character reader (OCR)

An optical character reader recognises the shape of characters and numbers and works out what the characters represent. Therefore, pages from a book can be scanned using OCR software and converted into text in a word processing program. An example of the use of an OCR is in a hospital registration department. The new patient completes a handwritten form with their details and the form is passed through an OCR which reads the data and enters it into the computer. It is therefore very important that the data is entered on the form in exactly the right spaces, otherwise the scanner will not find it.

Advantages of optical character reading:

- It is rapid.
- It interprets handwriting as well as typeface.

Disadvantages of optical character reading:

- Because of the huge variety in people's handwriting, it can make errors in recognising the shape of letters. In the example below, will this be read as an 'h' or an 'n'?

Task 10.2

One of the main problems with optical character recognition at present is that it sometimes has difficulty in recognising similar shaped characters and numbers, such as P and 8, or G and Q, when they are handwritten. Write down four more sets of letters or numbers that could easily be confused.

Magnetic Ink Character Recognition (MICR)

Another method of automated data capture is Magnetic Ink Character Recognition (MICR). All banks and building societies use MICR for processing cheques. The numbers on the bottom of a cheque are printed in special characters in magnetic ink and represent the number of the cheque, the number of the branch or the Sort Code and the customer's account number. When the customer has completed the amount details and the cheque has been handed into the bank, the amount shown on the cheque is also printed on the bottom, again using magnetic ink and an encoder.

The cheques are then processed using a magnetic reader which reads and stores the data.

See the example below.

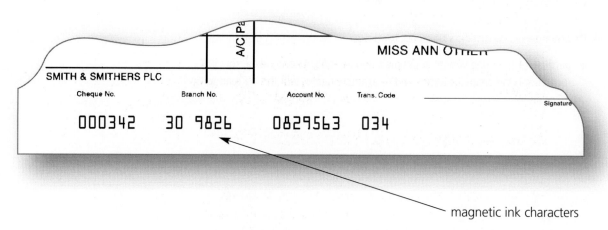

magnetic ink characters

Advantages of MICR are:

- It is hard to forge the characters.

- The characters can still be read even if the cheque is dirty or crumpled.

- The data is transferred directly into the accounting system of the bank.

Disadvantages of MICR are:

- Errors can be made when the cheque amount is added.

- MICR readers and encoders are very expensive.

If a bank or building society cheque is dirty or torn, how do you think the data contained in the magnetic characters is entered into the computer?

Electronic Point of Sale (EPOS)

Nearly everything we buy nowadays has a barcode on it. This is a set of thick and thin parallel lines, which represent a 13 digit number that is usually also printed above or below the bar. The coded number identifies the product uniquely and indicates the country of origin, the company that made the product, the product code number and package size. The last digit is a check digit that acts as an accuracy check to ensure that the barcode is read or keyed in correctly. The barcode does not include the price of the product because these frequently change.

We will look at how barcodes are used in a supermarket. A customer goes round the shop loading their trolley and then takes it to a checkout point. The goods are passed over a laser scanner that reads the barcodes. The scanner is linked to an Electronic Point of Sale Terminal (EPOS) that has a keyboard, a screen and a small dot matrix printer built into it (see Unit 12). The data from the barcode is sent to the store's main computer which immediately returns information about the product name and price to the checkout, where they are printed on the customer's receipt and the amount added to the total.

The same details also appear on the screen of the EPOS. Sometimes the scanner cannot read the barcode, so the numbers are keyed into the EPOS using the keyboard. When all the goods have been recorded, the EPOS produces an itemised receipt for the customer showing the names and prices of all the products, the total amount to be paid, the date and time etc.

All the checkouts in the supermarket are linked to the main computer and this records all the items that have been sold. Details about the amount of stock held in the shop's warehouse are also recorded in a stock control file. At the end of each day, the main computer produces a report showing the total amount that has been sold of each item and this number is subtracted from the overall amount recorded in the stock control file. If any item has dropped below the re-order level, an order will be sent for the required goods, with the shop or departmental manager deciding how much stock should be ordered.

In the case of goods that are frequently bought, such as bread and milk, the re-ordering is usually done automatically. As soon as the goods in stock drop below the re-order level, an order is sent immediately to the supplier via e-mail or EDI (Electronic Data Interchange), asking for a pre-set number of items.

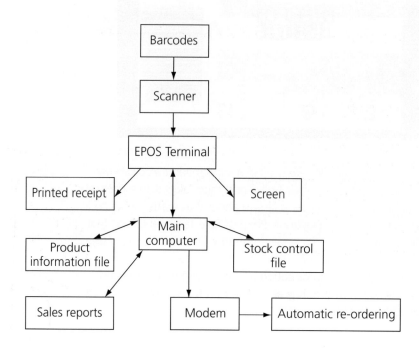

The diagram below shows the process of an EPOS system.

Advantages of Electronic Point of Sale Terminals:

■ Barcode scanners are much more accurate than manual entry of prices.

■ Barcodes and scanners make passing through the checkouts quicker for customers.

■ Fast-selling items can be monitored easily and restocked to meet demand.

Disadvantages of Electronic Point of Sale Terminals:

■ Customers have to be informed of prices by labelling on the shelves.

■ The system is expensive to set up for small retailers.

It is not only supermarkets that make use of barcodes for data capture. Examples of other types of use include:

■ hospitals and doctors surgeries – barcodes are used to identify samples taken from patients.

■ road freight – goods sent by road are often marked with barcodes, which enables the exact location of a package to be traced at any time during its journey.

Task 10.4

1 We have looked at some of the uses of barcodes. See if you can find two other examples.

2 Explain how they are used and what data is contained in the bars.

Magnetic stripe cards

A magnetic stripe is a short length of magnetic tape sealed into the surface of a ticket or card. The stripe is encoded with information that identifies the owner or user. The card is 'swiped' across a reader and the stripe is read, which is why this type of card is sometimes called a 'swipe' card.

We will look at some of the ways in which swipe cards are used.

Bank cards

When a customer wishes to take some cash out of their bank account, they often use an Automatic Telling Machine (ATM), also known as a

cashpoint machine. These are located in the wall outside banks, building societies and in public places such as stations, airports and supermarkets. The customer inserts their magnetic stripe card into the ATM. The magnetic stripe on the card has details of their bank code, account number and the expiry date of the card stored in it. A Personal Identification Number (PIN) also has to be entered by the customer; this is checked by the machine and has to match the card. The customer then chooses the service they require and if they want to withdraw money, keys in the amount required. As long as there are sufficient funds in the account, the cash and the card are returned to the customer.

Task 10.5

1 What measures can a bank or building society take to stop you withdrawing more money than you have in your account?

2 What do you think may happen if you enter an incorrect PIN into an ATM machine three times?

3 Why might this be to your advantage in the long term?

Debit cards

Many people pay for goods in shops by using a debit card instead of a cheque or cash. The card is swiped through an Electronic Fund Transfer at Point of Sale Terminal (EFTPOS), which is similar to an EPOS Terminal with additional features. The details of the sale and the card are stored in the terminal.

If a purchase is over a certain amount, the terminal connects to a Wide Area Network called SwitchNet to make sure the customer has enough money in their account to pay for the goods; this takes about five seconds. For smaller purchases, the details are stored in the terminal until the end of the working day and sent to the retailer's bank each night. The retailer's account is then credited with the amount due much more quickly than through the cheque system. Details are also sent to the customer's bank so that the amount due is deducted from their account.

Credit cards

This is another use of magnetic stripe cards, which allows a customer to have instant credit. Again, the card is 'swiped' through a terminal, which is linked to the retailer's bank and the credit card company. The customer's credit card account is checked to ensure that there is enough credit available to make the purchase and that the card is valid and has not been reported as having been lost or stolen. If all is well, the credit card company issues an authorisation for the purchase to go ahead and the credit card company pays the retailer. The customer receives a statement at the end of each month telling him/her how much they owe the credit card company.

Phonecards

Magnetic stripe cards are also used as phonecards. Phonecards are purchased for set amounts of money, eg £5 or £10, and this buys credits for the card user. The amount of credits available is stored on the magnetic stripe and as the card is used the number of credits reduces until the card runs out.

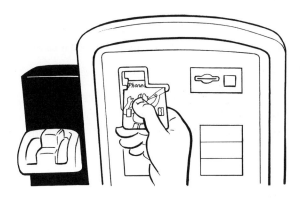

The main advantages of this type of card are:

■ They make transferring money and other transactions much quicker.

■ They are cheap and simple to produce.

■ In many instances, they replace the use of cash, which is safer for the customer.

Disadvantages of magnetic stripe cards:

- If the cards are stolen or lost, they can be used fraudulently.

- They can be damaged by scratching, which makes them unusable.

- Magnetic fields can erase or change the data.

Verification

The electronic methods of data capture that we have looked at are generally reliable, but no method can be completely accurate. Inaccuracies can be caused by:

- an error in processing the data because of a mistake in the programming

- an error that occurs when data is sent from one computer to another because of a poor connection

- data from forms etc being input incorrectly because of typing errors

- the operator or scanner finding it difficult to interpret the handwriting.

It is important that errors are avoided as far as possible, so organisations work out procedures to test the validity of the data they have captured. These testing systems could include:

- comparing the actual results with the expected results to see if they match

- inputting the same data twice to ensure that it is exactly the same and therefore correct

- checking that the data captured is sensible

- checking that the data is in the correct format – should it be numeric or alphanumeric?

All these checks are programmed into the computer and, if any of the errors mentioned above occur, the computer informs the user who can then investigate the error and make the necessary corrections.

When data has been captured and stored using any of the methods we have looked at in this unit, it needs to be protected and kept secure. Various methods of maintaining security and backing up the data in case it gets damaged or corrupted in some way will be discussed in Unit 17.

Revision Questions

1 What is the most commonly used method for inputting text-based data?

mouse   joy-stick   keyboard   microphone

2 An optical mark reader detects .... when they have been made on a specially designed form?

ticks   crosses   marks   grades

3 .... recognises the shape of characters and numbers?

OMR   OCR   ATM   PIN

4 A barcode is a set of lines of different thicknesses that are ....

parallel   diagonal   identical   horizontal

5 When all the goods have been scanned, an **EPOS** Terminal produces an itemised ....

bill   receipt   credit note   debit note

6 In a stock control file, the overall amount of stock recorded as held has the items sold during the day ....

added to it   subtracted from it   divided by it   multiplied by it

7 An MICR is used by banks and building societies for processing ....

cheques   standing orders   direct debits   cash

8 Magnetic stripe cards are also called ....

stripe cards   swipe cards   swing cards   ribbon cards

9 To withdraw cash from an ATM the customer has to key in a ....

Personal Identification number   National Insurance number   bank account number   National Health Number

10 When used to make a phone call, phonecards use up ....

debits   cash   credits   money

Task 10.6

Visit a supermarket that uses EPOS Terminals and scanners. Try to find out what happens when goods that do not already have a barcode on them, arrive in the supermarket, for example, fresh fruit and vegetables. How are the details for these goods entered into the computer?

Task 10.7

Find out all you can about SMART cards and write a paragraph about how they are used and where they are likely to be used.

 xtension task

Happy Ideas Ltd uses questionnaires to find out what customers want and what makes them buy its products.

1   Consider ONE advantage of using a postal questionnaire for this purpose.   (4 marks)

2   Why might Happy Ideas Ltd first test the postal questionnaire on a small number of customers?   (2 marks)

DATA GATHERING, RECORDING AND PRESENTATION SYSTEMS

PRESENTATION

At the end of this unit you should be able to:

▶ understand the different types of presentation

▶ match presentational style to audience needs

▶ understand the purpose of giving and obtaining information

▶ understand the importance and impact of the presentation.

PRESENTATION TYPES

There are many different types of presentations; they can be in written, numerical, oral or visual format.

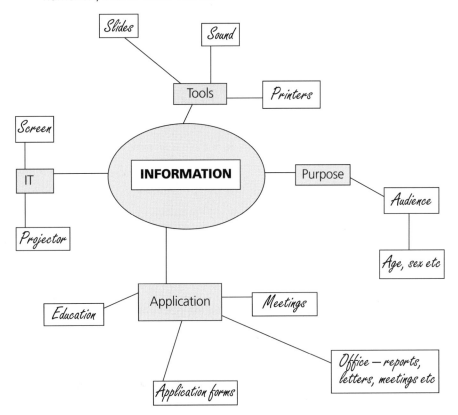

Task 11.1

Make a list of the times you can think of when a presentation may be needed. Then place your list into columns – personal and office.

Written

The written format is used in all situations. A note left for someone to carry out a task or a letter sent to a company to complain about a service or product not received, or a memo, fax, report etc, all of these can be either handwritten:

I am writing to complain

or they can be word-processed:

The text in this book has been word-processed.

The problems with handwritten work are:

- the person's handwriting may not be readable
- the time taken to write the message out
- there could be spelling or grammatical errors
- it is difficult to transfer the information, ie word-processed information can be passed from one person to another by disk or e-mail.
- if there is an error then the whole piece may have to be rewritten.

The advantage of word processed work is that it eliminates some of the above problems.

Task 11.2

Test the above out – choose a piece of text. Have one person write the text out and another person word process the text. Which was easier? Which caused the most problem? Which looks more effective? Why?

Numerical

Numerical presentation is using numbers, eg 1, 2, 3 or roman numerals I, II, III, in fact anything that contains figures. Many tables and charts may be used in presenting numbers.

Unit 9 goes into detail with regard to how useful charts and diagrams can be to illustrate points, which will enable your audience to understand.

Oral

Orally presenting information is when someone is giving a speech or talk or lecture. Any time someone is talking they are orally communicating. Each lesson, teachers are constantly giving oral presentations.

Can you remember what was said in Unit 9 about oral communication? Know your subject matter well, know exactly what you are going to say, do not speak too quietly or too quickly. Refer back to Unit 9 if you have forgotten.

Task 11.3

Make notes on the different ways four of your teachers present a lesson. Do they change their tone of their voice, do they raise or lower the pitch, do they always keep their eyes on their audience, or are they often referring to notes? Some people often need props, such as something to hold or occasionally writing on the board. Display the above information in a table.

Visual

Visual presentation is when someone uses charts, projectors, slides etc to demonstrate something or to inform (see Unit 9 People). Many companies are now using more sophisticated presentations because the advancement in computer technology has allowed people to enhance their work. You have already learned that pictures are a more effective way of presenting information – a well-known phrase is 'a picture can say a thousand words'.

An example of this is a company who manufacturers cars – Jay Cars. They have to give their sales outlets and potential customers details of the new model of car they are producing. A few years ago the company would have had to use the services of an advertising agency and asked them to produce something for the company. They would have had to pay the agency a considerable fee for this work. Today, the company would employ its own staff, who are capable of using IT equipment, such as scanners and computer aided design (CAD). These people create drawings on the computer. Special equipment is purchased that allows acetate slides to be printed and information to be displayed on large screen monitors. If all this work were sent out to the agency, then the cost would probably be nearly £250,000 a year. By employing these people in-house, the company would probably save themselves about £100,000.

Many companies are now equipping their sales staff with computers so that they can use the machines to call up prepared material, which could be charts and sales literature.

You have already learned that pictures are more able to communicate ideas and concepts to an audience better than the written or spoken word.

Visual aids are normally used to reinforce what is being said by the presenter. If the work is displayed attractively, then the audience will be more able to digest the key points. Colour is also an important part of a visual presentation because it catches the person's attention and hopefully maintains their interest.

CAD is used by engineers, designers, architects etc and has replaced the traditional drawing boards that were used to produce drawings/ diagrams. The drawings/diagrams they can produce are things like plans for a new kitchen, conservatory or bedroom, houses, new cars and maps to name a few. CAD drawings/diagrams are much easier to create and change than the old method of drawing by hand. Before CAD, if an alteration was made, then it had to be redrawn – there was no other way of changing the work (see Unit 4 Electronic).

Task 11.4

You have been asked by a local company to list the advantages and disadvantages of the following types of presentation:

- oral
- visual
- written
- numerical.

State which presentation method you would use for the following and why:

- design of a new bathroom
- importance of safety while walking in a busy town
- details of how you see the performance of the company over the next five years.

MATCHING PRESENTATION STYLE TO AUDIENCE NEEDS

Age

It is very important that you are always aware of who your audience is. For example, the type of information you would use for young children may be very different to what you would use for adults.

Task 11.5

You work for a local printing company and have been asked to design and print a ticket for the following:

- a school disco for Year 6 pupils
- a school concert highlighting the award-winning school band
- the old-aged pensioners' Christmas party
- a local church garden fête.

Explain your reasons for designing the tickets the way you have.

Gender

Advertising companies are very conscious of the power they have selling a product by making sure that their advert is aimed at the different sexes. Men may want to buy a product because it has a picture of a famous footballer on, whereas women might be more interested if it has a famous film star on it. Therefore, when giving a presentation of any kind, consideration must be given to the gender of the audience.

Task 11.6

Collect a selection of advertisements that you think typically depict different genders. Then compare those for women to those for men.

Discuss why you think they are different.

Topic

The topic for a presentation could also have an effect on how the presentation is delivered. For example, if the topic was on children's clothes, then you would want to use pictures/slides of young children. A more visual effect would be to have some real children wearing the clothes. This would be presenting the information in the best possible way. It would have more impact on the audience than just describing the clothes or showing pictures.

Subject matter

Again, this is very similar to topic and the presenter should take great care to ensure that the subject matter is relevant to the audience, as well as being pitched at the correct level.

Status

This is particularly important when giving a presentation of any kind. You must take into consideration the status of the audience. A group of Directors of a company would expect a presentation to be to the point and of a very high standard; every single item prepared and well presented with no hiccups of any kind. Time would be of the essence to them and they would not expect to have to sit through a long and tedious presentation that never quite got to the subject. In contrast to this, a presentation given by a group of pupils on their recent work experience would certainly not be up to the same standard. The pupils may not have given a presentation before or know exactly what is expected of them, so their skills on what to use and how to talk to the audience would be more basic.

PURPOSE OF A PRESENTATION

Giving information

A number of presentations are used as a means of giving information. If a company is introducing a new product, then the presentation they will be giving is to inform its audience of the new product. Thus they are giving information.

Obtaining information

On the other hand, when people attend a conference on a specific subject, for example a teacher wishing to update their knowledge on a particular GCSE course, they are actually obtaining information. They want the presenter to inform them of the changes that have taken place. They have some prior knowledge of the subject.

Expressing opinions

Most presentations will allow for the audience to ask questions or the presenter may ask questions of those people at the meeting. This is an opportunity for everyone to give their opinion on what is being discussed or their points of view on the subject of the presentation. An example of this might be a meeting about planning permission for someone to build houses on a piece of land near a village. There will be some people who believe that permission should not be granted and there will also be those people who believe it should be. Everyone has a right to express their own opinion but must also allow others to give their opinion.

Exchanging ideas

Exchanging ideas is also similar to expressing opinions – the difference here is that both sides will take on board the other person's point of view. An example of this might be at a local Gardeners Club meeting or presentation. One person will give their ideas on how something should be grown in the garden and the best way to nurture the plants, while other people may believe that what they do is the best way. In this situation, what will happen is that both keen gardeners will probably try each other's method out and then find which one suits them the best. They are really exchanging one idea for another.

Presenting arguments

Politicians are renowned for presenting their arguments in a manner that would make you believe that their proposal/belief is the best and correct way. If the opportunity arises, listen to a party political broadcast. Listen to how they put forward their opinions and arguments, quite often they will try and baffle the audience with facts and figures to make you believe that what they will do is correct and the other party is incorrect.

A good argument should give both points of view with a final summary of which side of the argument they truly believe in.

THE IMPORTANCE AND IMPACT OF THE PRESENTATION

This is probably the most important part of any presentation. This is what the audience will remember – were there any spelling mistakes, was it clearly presented, was it effective, was it too long and people fell asleep?

Spelling

Most modern word processing packages will have a dictionary against which the words in a document can be compared to check their spelling. You are often allowed to add words to the dictionary, this is especially useful if you use specialist terms in subjects such as medicine and education. It is important to remember that spellchecks will not remove an error, they will only suggest a word for something they do not recognise in their dictionary. An example of this is if you typed in the word 'he' instead of the word 'the' – the spellcheck would not detect an error as 'he' is a word that it understands and is in the dictionary. Therefore, it is imperative to proofread your work very carefully as well.

Task 11.7

Spot the errors in the following document.

STOP WIND DAMAGE NOW!

1 The Tunnel Effect

Spaces between houses act like wind tunnels and cause wind to speed up – it's no wonder the shrub by your bank gate never came to anything. Even when it might not seem windy, there's away a breeze whistling between buildings and frying out containers. Fit a gate that's made of trellis or a trellis-like material, rather than a solid one; this helps to filter the wild and snow it down. Grow tough low-growers, such as alpines, where the wind is at its strongest or even avoid planting altogether in there spots.

Punctuation

Many people nowadays use incorrect punctuation. Common errors are putting the apostrophe in the wrong place. For example, 'theres'' should read 'there is' or 'there's'. Similar to spelling errors, the computer software may well recognise a majority of the errors.

Grammar

Grammar is also an important factor when giving a presentation. Most computer programs will have a feature that checks grammar. This is certainly very useful if your English is not very good. Similar to punctuation and spelling, grammar checkers do have their limitations. As yet they find only a few faults and do tend to provide an incorrect analysis of the grammar of writing. You must always exercise care when using this facility on a computer as they are not always correct.

For example:

We <u>was</u> going to the cinema the other day when a terrible thing happened.

Clarity

Clarity means clearness of speech. To speak with clarity means to speak clearly and slowly enough so that the audience can hear and understand what is being said. Remember the larger the room the slightly slower one has to speak so that the voice will travel the length of the room. Those people in the back of the room want to hear what is being said otherwise they will lose interest.

Quality of outcome

Quality of outcome is the actual appearance of the whole presentation. Is it presented well, does the presenter look rushed? Panicky? Are they prepared for the audience? Is the quality of the work worth reading and looking at? These are all questions one should ask of a presentation. The more prepared it is, both in the handouts and quality of the presentation, the more likely it is to have a better outcome. Every presenter wants their audience going away with the opinion that they have gained something from the presentation and it was worth their time and money.

Effectiveness

This also applies – it is the same as quality of outcome. A presentation will be effective if it is well presented.

Task 11.8

You are an experienced presenter giving numerous presentations to many different audiences. You have been asked by someone who has never done a presentation before to write a checklist of the jobs that have to be done – so that they can have a presentation that will incorporate all the above points. Write this checklist.

twelve

MONEY TRANSFER SYSTEMS

PAYMENT SYSTEMS

At the end of this unit you should understand:

▶ what methods of payment systems businesses can use

▶ how businesses transfer payments to each other

▶ why they use different methods of payment.

Most businesses exist to make a profit. To do this they sell goods or services at a higher price than it cost to produce them. A decision has to be made on how to transfer payment from the buyer to the seller.

CASH

One method of transferring payment is to use cash. In this system of payment, the buyer would meet the seller and agree a price for the goods or service and then money in the form of coins and notes would be passed between them. This is a straightforward system that is easy to use and understand. However, if a large sum of money has to be paid then this can cause problems as follows:

■ carrying large amounts of money is awkward and uncomfortable

■ the risk of the money being stolen is greater

■ there is a danger of accepting forged bank notes.

CHEQUES

Not many businesses today ask to be paid in cash for the reasons on the previous page. A safer method of payment is by cheque. A cheque is a written order by an account holder (the person who wrote the cheque) to his/her bank to pay a specified sum of money to the account of the person or business whose name is written on the cheque.

Each day millions of cheques are cashed and without the use of computers this would be an impossible task. All banks and building societies keep a record of their customers' accounts (how much money a business or person has in their bank/building society) on a mainframe computer. These mainframes keep a record of all transactions and update accounts as withdrawals (money taken out) and deposits (money paid in) are made.

All banks and building societies are in a clearing system and their mainframes are connected. All cheques must go through this clearing system. This involves the sending and settlement of payments between accounts held at different banks and different branches of the same bank.

This process takes three days but would be a great deal slower if it were not for computers. The key to processing so much information lies in the coded characters at the bottom of the cheque which are printed in magnetic ink.

Three sets of numbers are encoded in magnetic ink on the cheque:

■ the customer's account number

■ the sort code – each branch of every bank or building society has its own unique number

■ the cheque number.

Using a Magnetic Ink Character Reader (MICR) (see Unit 10), a great number of cheques can be read into a computer at a great speed. The computer can then sort the cheques into the various banks and branches and send the details of all the amounts to be added and deducted from customers' accounts to the different banks' computers.

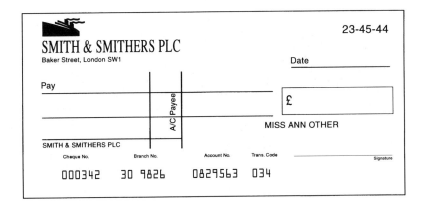

The disadvantages of this method of payment are:

■ the time it takes to clear cheques and therefore get paid

■ the wrong amount or name could be written on the cheque

■ the wrong information could be encoded onto the cheque.

If there are any errors or mistakes on a cheque it is usually sent back to the person or business writing the cheque for them to make any amendments or corrections. This can be embarrassing for the drawer (person who wrote the cheque). It also takes time and means payment of the amount on the cheque is delayed, so it is important cheques sent and received are checked carefully.

If there are mistakes on the cheque and it is paid into the bank, it will be returned three or four days later, which again means payment of the cheque is delayed.

The most common errors on cheques are a missing signature, the payee's name is missing (the person to whom the cheque is made out), the words and figures do not agree, the date is missing or any alterations are not initialled.

To safeguard against problems of security when paying by cheque, the following should be remembered:

■ always write in ink

■ put your initials against any alteration

■ draw a line through any spaces left.

As an additional safeguard against fraud most businesses also insist on two people signing the cheque and, when receiving a cheque from private individuals and not business customers, that the number of the cheque guarantee card is written on the back of the cheque.

Task 12.1

1 Use suitable software to design a cheque OR your teacher will give you copies.

2 Complete the following cheques adding all the information you think necessary. Use today's date and your own signature.

    a) P White needs payment for goods he supplied costing £183.70.   **(4 marks)**

    b) You need to pay Mrs H Walker for stationery supplies costing £63.90.   **(4 marks)**

3 What is the person signing a cheque called?   **(1 mark)**

4 What is the person receiving a cheque called?   **(1 mark)**

5 List three reasons why a cheque may be rejected by the bank. Explain the implications to the business if this happens.   **(9 marks)**

Other ways in which banks or building societies help their business customers to make payments are by credit transfer, standing orders and direct debits.

PAYING-IN SLIP

Businesses receive cash and cheques in payment for selling their goods or services. They need to pay these into their bank and to do this they use a paying-in slip. This is also known as a bank giro credit or credit transfer.

Personal customers may have paying-in slips in the back of their cheque books. Business customers usually have a paying-in book consisting only of paying-in slips.

Task 12.2

1 Try and collect a variety of paying-in slips from your local banks.

2 Complete one paying-in slip with all the following payments:

Cheques		Cash
W Galvin	£35.00	2 × £50
M Hughes	£42.00	3 × £20
HBC	£120.00	6 × £10
F Coghan	£90.00	12 × £1
		27 × 50p
		12 × 20p
		2 × 10p
		bronze £3.00

STANDING ORDER

Businesses may have to pay fixed amounts on a regular basis, for example loan repayments, business rates or insurance premiums. A standing order is an instruction to their bank to make these regular payments. The bank will programme its computer to make the payment as instructed providing there is money in the account. This means the payment is not forgotten and it saves having to write out a cheque every time.

DIRECT DEBIT

A direct debit is similar to a standing order in that it instructs the bank to make regular payments from one account to another. The difference is that the exact amount of money that is to be paid is not specified. For example, a manufacturing business may not know how much electricity it will use from month to month. It will sign a direct debit with the electricity company to allow the electricity company to withdraw the payment for the amount of electricity used. This means that the business receiving the payment can vary the amount but it must inform the account holder first.

Like standing orders, direct debits allow business customers to pay bills easily and conveniently, saving time and trouble in writing and sending cheques or paying by cash. Using these methods also helps in managing a business' cash flow as the business knows exactly when cash is flowing in and out of their accounts.

BANKERS AUTOMATED CLEARING SYSTEM (BACS)

All of the above methods of payment involve paper somewhere in the process. As computers become more sophisticated, paper is being used less and less in the system of transferring payments between buyers and sellers. Banks are increasingly using a payment system called **Electronic Funds Transfer** (EFT) to make payments between account holders.

An example of such a system is BACS. This is a similar system to the cheque clearing system but instead of the information being written on a cheque the information is electronically transferred from one bank's computer to another via a telephone link. It is an electronic payment system that allows the business customers of banks to make payments to individuals or to other businesses. A business will obtain the banking details of a regular supplier and instead of sending a cheque will get its bank to transfer the money from its account to the regular supplier's account through the computer.

The use of BACS has revolutionised the payments industry and enables more companies than ever to utilise the benefits of making automated payments because:

- bank accounts are updated straightaway
- there is no need to use cash or wait for cheques to clear
- it is reliable as computers will not make mistakes over the amounts to be paid
- it is convenient because there is no longer the need to make trips to the bank.

The BACS system is used by an enormous number of companies to pay monthly salaries directly into employees' accounts. It is also used to pay direct debits, standing orders, mortgages and most types of regular bills.

Other examples of electronic funds transfer are **debit cards**, **credit cards** and **smart cards**, which are commonly known as 'plastic' – which we have discussed in greater detail in Unit 10.

DEBIT CARD

With these cards money is transferred electronically from one account to another. Debit cards, such as Switch and Delta, are cards that are linked

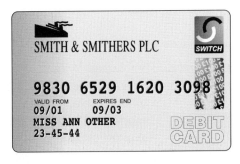

to a bank or building society account. They are used as an alternative to cheques.

The information about the card holder is held on the magnetic stripe and these cards work the same way for businesses as they do for individuals.

If you use your debit card to pay for an item in a shop, your card will be swiped through a magnetic stripe reader, which will then contact your bank's computer through the telephone network to make sure you have enough money in your account to make the payment. If you do, the money will be transferred electronically between the shop's computer and your bank account.

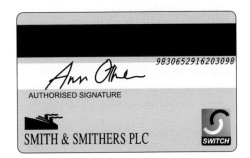

The computerised till is known as **point of sale** (POS) and the transfer of funds is called **electronic funds transfer at point of sale** (EFTPOS).

Today, debit cards are multi-functional in that they act as automatic teller machine (ATM) cards, which allow you to withdraw cash from dispensers and they act as cheque guarantee cards as well.

CREDIT CARD

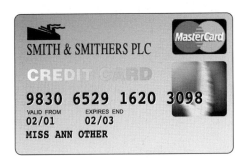

Credit cards, such as Visa and Mastercard, work in the same way as debit cards but they enable the holder to make purchases and to draw cash out of the credit company's account up to an agreed limit. The amount spent on the card can be settled in full, usually by the end of the month or in part payments. If the holder has not paid off the full amount, they have to pay interest on the remaining balance.

SMART CARD

A smart card is similar to a credit or debit card but instead of the information being held on a magnetic stripe it is on a computer chip,

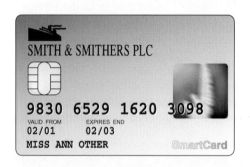

which enables it to store much more information. A smart card performs the same functions of a debit or credit card but it can also store money electronically in the chip, a bit like an electronic purse.

The smart card can hold details of the holder's credit limit and carry a record of the transactions made within this limit. The card holder can replace the funds that have been taken out at a later date by placing their card in a terminal, which deposits the funds on to the chip.

Money is transferred from one smart card to another, 'chip to chip'. To unlock the card a PIN number is needed. This is a personal identification number that is unique to its owner. When goods or services are purchased, the card is placed in the terminal, which has its own smart card inside it and the money is transferred from one card to another.

The advantages of these cards are:

- they are easy to use as payment is immediate just like cash

- they are flexible as amounts can be transferred by telephone or payment can be made person to person

- they are convenient because cash machines and telephones give more access points

- they are safer because they are more difficult to access and forge than magnetic stripe cards.

The main disadvantage of using smart cards is the cost involved. Many automatic teller machines (ATMs) and EPOS would have to be converted to be able to read smart cards. For this reason they are not so popular in this country but are used extensively in banking systems in Europe and in particular France.

However, many businesses give their staff these cards to pay for goods or services or to pay expenses. These may be known as business, company or corporate cards.

Task 12.3

Visit your local bank or building society and find out about the different types of cards they offer. When you have collected this information try to answer the following:

1 What do each of the cards offer and how do they differ?

2 What is the interest rate charged on each card?

3 If you had to choose one of these cards, which one would it be and why?

Prepare a presentation of your findings for your class.

ELECTONIC DATA INTERCHANGE (EDI)

This is a system where data relating to business can be exchanged via any electronic messaging service. A business can send an order for new stock to a supplier from its computer terminal to the supplier's computer. The supplier delivers the stock and sends an invoice for the amount they are owed from its computer to the buyer's computer. The buyer can then authorise its bank to make payment to the supplier's bank. No paper is involved.

For this system to work businesses who are connected to the system must all have the same standard documents. The advantages of this system are:

■ is less expensive and faster than sending orders by post, phone or fax

■ reduces errors, such as lost or wrongly printed orders

■ means no paperwork is required

■ means invoices are paid promptly and businesses receive their money immediately without waiting for cheques to clear

■ allows businesses to keep their financial records up to date and predict cashflow more accurately

■ reduces bank charges.

TELEBANKING

With the exception of cash, any business transaction where payment is involved means that money has to be transferred from the buyer's account to the seller's bank account. As we have already seen there are a number of ways to do this but, as communication technology improves, it is now possible for individuals and businesses to access their accounts from their home or office via their telephone.

Many banks operate a 24-hour service where customers can get information about their account and carry out various transactions, from paying bills to cancelling direct debits, when it suits them for the cost of a local call. Customers can access their accounts through talking to an adviser or using the push buttons on their telephone.

INTERNET BANKING

Account holders can now conduct their banking business through the Internet. This gives secure 24-hour access to their account from their workplace or home by computer. This gives them the same services as telebanking, that is paying bills, setting up, amending or cancelling standing orders and direct debits, switching money from their bank account to someone else's instantly, but also allows the customer to view the information.

The advantages of doing business this way are:

- you can access without having to go to the bank or wait for statements in the post

- no paper is involved which saves on administration costs

- you can keep a constant track of all your transactions

- you can keep accounts up to date and monitor your cash flow situation.

The one big worry people have with this type of banking, however, is that someone may access their bank account, so security is of vital importance. Most banks require a password, a passcode and they use the latest encryption technology so no-one can access customer accounts. Encryption means to encode any data in such a way that it is unreadable to anyone who does not know how to decode the data.

Task 12.4

Using suitable software, prepare a poster for a local bank that will encourage its customers to change to its Internet banking services.

E-COMMERCE

E-commerce is seen by many as the new Industrial Revolution and many people believe that any business that does not get online will be left behind by their competitors who do get online.

Over the last ten years the number of people buying and selling on the Internet has increased. The way it works is that businesses put details of their products on their websites. Customers can then browse through either a particular product range to see who offers the best deal or through the products of a particular business. If a customer wishes to buy a product they can order it online and pay using their credit or debit card.

Encryption software converts the card details into a code so that the details cannot be stolen and unauthorised purchases made. Once the products have been ordered and paid for they are then delivered. The most popular online shopping products are books, music, holidays and foodstuffs.

The advantages to businesses in selling this way are:

- small firms that produce specialist goods can sell their products anywhere in the world thus increasing their market

- costs can be reduced because the cost of downloading information is paid for by the Internet user not the provider, so things like sales brochures no longer need to be produced

- sales staff are no longer needed as the information is online instead.

One problem that online businesses have to overcome is the user's fear that the company they are dealing with might not be trustworthy. People prefer to deal with businesses they know and trust, so it is important for online businesses to build up a good reputation by providing a quality service.

Task 12.5

Try and find out the names of as many businesses as you can that offer online shopping. Include their online addresses and what they sell.

Revision Questions

1 Which of the following methods of payment would you use if a shop did not have an electronic terminal?

debit card   credit card   receipt   cash

2 A written order from an account holder to their bank to pay a specified sum of money to the named recipient is a ....

cheque   standing order   direct debit   paying-in slip

3 Which of the following, found on a cheque, is the unique number that identifies a particular bank and branch of that bank?

account number   sort code   cheque number   date

4 If you wished to pay cheques/cash personally into a bank account you would use a
....

direct debit   paying-in slip   cheque   standing order

5 An instruction to the bank to pay a fixed amount on a regular basis to a specified person or business is a ....

direct debit   cheque   credit slip   standing order

6 The information about a debit card holder is held on a ....

magnetic strip   computer chip   hologram   receipt

7 A card that holds details of the holder on a computer chip is a ....

credit card   smart card   debit card   ATM card

8 What does EFT stand for?

A electronic finance transaction   B electronic funds transaction   C electronic funds transfer
D electronic finance transfer

9 What works by exchanging standard message formats between businesses via any electronic messaging service?

BACS   EFT   EDI   EFTPOS

10 Online shopping takes place through the ....

telephone   Internet   television   telex

Task 12.6

1 Look at the list below and say which method(s) of payment you would use for each.

- milk, bread and butter from a local shop
- the deposit for a house
- the repayments on a loan
- paying for a holiday bought over the Internet
- an employer paying an employee's monthly salary
- a supermarket paying its supplier of baked beans.

2 Give reasons to support your choices.   (10 marks)

Extension task

Explain the advantages and disadvantages of using credit cards and debit cards instead of cash:

- to a business
- to a customer of the business.   (10 marks)

MONEY TRANSFER SYSTEMS

BUSINESS DOCUMENTS

> **At the end of this unit you should understand:**
>
> ▸ what documents businesses use
>
> ▸ why businesses use documents
>
> ▸ how these documents are used in business transactions.

BUSINESS TRANSACTIONS

Before a business can sell its goods and services it has to make sure that it has a system in place that will record its various transactions. A large business may have thousands of customers so it is important that it keeps a record of all its transactions.

When a transaction takes place a record will nearly always be made. This can be either on paper or on computer. The main reasons for this are:

- to create evidence of the transaction, as the records provide a permanent record, which can be referred to in the future if anything needs to be checked. You cannot always rely on people's memories!

- to ensure that bills are paid on time and debts (money owed) are collected

- to show how the business is doing – is it making a profit?

- to provide the Inland Revenue with the information they need to assess the tax liability of the company

- to enable the Customs and Excise office to assess the VAT owed.

Each firm will design and use its own forms and documents but they will all include certain features.

Below is a diagram that shows the documents that are produced during a typical business transaction.

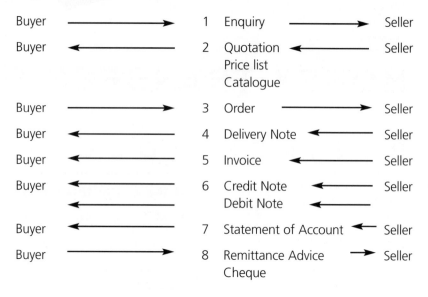

The above diagram is complicated so to help you understand this process and learn what each document is you are going to complete a number of tasks based around a case study.

CASE STUDY – THE SCHOOL OFFICE

Your school is a business like any other and is involved in many business transactions, from buying coloured pencils to buying computers. To help you understand the diagram above you are going to imagine that you work in the school office. You are going to go through the same process from beginning to end by buying textbooks for the Business Studies department.

1 Enquiry

A buyer has to find out what a seller has to offer. This is generally done through a **letter of enquiry** in which the buyer asks the seller about prices and terms. Terms may include such things as:

■ whether the cost of delivery is included in the price – this is also known as carriage paid

■ any discounts that might be given for early payment or paying cash for the goods

■ trade discount that is given if a business is buying a large quantity of the goods.

The Headteacher
Nodlob School
Nodlob Lane
Newtown
NT6 5NL
Tel: 0191 635 789 – Fax 0191 643789

ENQUIRY TO Hodder and Strodder Abingdon Oxon OX14 4TD	DATE 4/4/01 ENQUIRY NUMBER Z23478 DELIVERY ADDRESS 78 Milton Park Oxon OX14 4TD

Please quote your price and delivery date for the following goods and services as specified:

Quantity	Description
30	Geography For You
20	History Lives

———————————— Signed

Task 13.1

1   Word process a letter of enquiry to a school book publisher.
    Your teacher will provide you with some names and addresses.

2   Are there any other ways in which you think you could have
    made an enquiry? Select the method you think is best and give
    your reasons.   (5 marks)

3   Why would a business send out more than one enquiry?
                                                            (3 marks)

2 Quotations, price lists or catalogues

As a result of the enquiry, the buyer will receive several quotations, price
lists or catalogues from the sellers.

A **quotation** states the goods available, the current price, delivery date and terms of payment.

A **catalogue** and **price list** are contained in a printed booklet, which gives details and illustrations of the goods, with or without prices, and is often sent with a quotation. A price list updates a catalogue to save the cost of reprinting the catalogue each time the prices change.

Task *13.2*

Using a book publisher's catalogue, select a textbook that would be useful to you in this subject. Calculate how much it would cost to buy one for every pupil in your class. Are there any special terms? What are they and why do you think you are offered them?

3 Order

After deciding on which product(s) to buy, the buyer will send an order form to the seller. The order form shows the quantity to be bought, the

Nodlob School			
Nodlob Lane			
Newtown			
NT6 5NL			
Tel: 0191 635789 – Fax: 0191 643789			

ORDER FORM
                                 Date   4 April 2001
                                 Order Number   47589

TO:
Hodder and Strodder
Abingdon
Oxon
OX 14 4TD

PLEASE SUPPLY AND DELIVER TO THE
ABOVE ADDRESS THE FOLLOWING GOODS

Description	Quantity	Unit Price	Total
Geography For You	**30**	**11.99**	**359.70**
History Lives	**20**	**13.99**	**279.80**

GOODS WILL ONLY BE ACCEPTED ON
PRODUCTION OF AN OFFICIAL ORDER NUMBER

Signed ....

type of product, a reference number, how much each product costs individually and how much the total cost is.

Each order form is numbered to tell it apart from others and copies are kept in case of any queries.

Using the order form in the book catalogue, write out an order for your textbooks.

4 Delivery note

This is sent with the goods by the seller. Details of the goods are given so that the buyer can check that the correct goods have been delivered. The buyer will have to sign the delivery note, which provides the seller with proof that the goods have been delivered.

Delivery notes can sometimes be called dispatch notes.

DELIVERY NOTE

Hodder and Strodder
78 Milton Park
Abingdon
Oxon
OX14 4TD
Tel: 01235 827722

Nodlob School Nodlob Lane Newtown NT6 5NL	Delivery Note No: 89076 Date: 4 April 01 Order No: 77003

Product Code	Quantity	Description
ISBN 5764 ISBN 8906	30 20	Geography For You History Lives

Signature ....   Name ....

---

5 Invoice

This is the main business document that shows all the details of the transaction and is sent by the seller. Although invoices produced by different businesses may vary, they will always show what items have been purchased, the quantity and price. It also shows the terms and the total price after discounts have been deducted and VAT added. The invoice can be checked against the order in case any mistakes have been made.

Suppliers usually give their customers 30–60 days to pay. The invoice may sometimes be sent in advance of the goods, with the goods, or it can be sent after the goods have been received.

Prices on invoices are often quoted before VAT is worked out. **Value Added Tax** is a tax on most goods and services and is currently at 17.5%. VAT is added to the price of the goods.

Buyers may receive goods from sellers at less than the advertised selling price. This may be because they have placed a bulk order or because they have paid promptly. This is known as **trade discount** and is always given as a percentage of the final price.

An invoice often has the abbreviation E and O E (errors and omissions excepted) printed on it, meaning that the invoice is correct apart from any errors or omissions. The purpose is to protect the supplier against loss from mistakes. For example, if a mistake has been made in

Hodder and Strodder
78 Milton Park
Abingdon
Oxon
OX14 4TD
Tel: 01235 827722
Fax: 0123 400454

INVOICE

Invoice: 652341
Date: 04/04/01
Customer ID: 55776

Bill To:
Nodlob School
Nodlob Lane
Newtown
NT6 5NL

Deliver To:
Same Address

Terms E&OE – 2.5% one month – 5% 7 days – carriage paid

Qty	Item	Description	Unit Pr	Total
30	ISBN 5764	GEOGRAPHY FOR YOU	11.99	359.70
20	ISBN 8906	HISTORY LIVES	13.99	279.80
1	ISBN 3847	TEACHER'S PACK HISTORY	40.00	40.00
			VAT 0%	
			Total	679.50

calculating the amount owing on the invoice, the supplier reserves the right to correct the mistake.

Task 13.4

You work for Hodder & Strodder, a book publisher that trades from 78 Milton Park, Abingdon, Oxon OX14 4TD. A customer, Nodlob School of Nodlob Lane, Newtown NT6 5NL, has ordered the following:

- 30 Business and Communication Systems textbooks at £10.99 each
  ISBN 0404 123456

- 1 Business and Communication Systems Teachers Resource Book at £40
  ISBN 0404 234567

- 20 Information Systems textbooks at £13.00 each
  ISBN 0404 345678

Carriage costs are £2.95 and a 5% cash discount is offered for full settlement if paid within 14 days. No VAT is paid on school textbooks.

Using suitable software create an invoice. Complete the invoice dated today, to be sent to the customer.

6 Credit note or debit note

These may be used to change amounts appearing on the invoice. This might happen if:

- some of the goods have been damaged and are returned
- not all of the goods have been received
- the unit price on the invoice is too high and the buyer has been overcharged.

A credit note is then issued by the seller to the buyer, which makes up the difference between what was paid for and what was actually received.

If the buyer receives more than they ordered or they were undercharged, the seller will send a debit note to the buyer for the extra amount that is owed. Some organisations prefer to deal with an undercharge or overcharge to a customer by sending a corrected invoice.

If used, the credit note will **reduce** the invoice amount. The debit note will **increase** the invoice amount.

CREDIT NOTE		**Hodder and Strodder** **78 Milton Park** **Abingdon** **Oxon OX14 4TD** **TEL: 01235 827722** **Fax: 0135 400454**		No. **667893**

Date/Tax point:
4/4/01

Quantity	Description	Catalogue Number	Unit Price £ p	Total Amount
5	History Lives	ISBN 8906	13 99	69.95
		Total excluding VAT		69.95
		VAT		
		Total credit		69.95

Reason for credit
Only 15 books delivered, 20 ordered

Task 13.5

Nodlob School only received 20 Business and Communication Systems textbooks. Which document would you now use and by how much would you have to credit/debit Nodlob School?

7 Statement of account

Payment for most business transactions is not required immediately and so the buyer is not expected to pay each invoice as it arrives.

When two companies do business regularly the seller will send a statement of account to the buyer. This is a document that shows the buyer's account with the seller and it is sent out to remind the buyer to pay their bill.

It shows the value of each invoice sent in a particular month, the payments that have been received from the buyer, any credit or debit notes and the unpaid balance. It is a summary of all the transactions that have taken place since the last statement was sent and shows whether there are any unpaid invoices.

Hodder and Strodder
78 Milton Park, Abingdon
Oxon, OX14 4TD
Tel: 01235 827722
Fax: 0135 400454

STATEMENT

Statement: 03765
Date: 4/4/01
Customer ID: 55776

Bill To:
Nodlob School
Nodlob Lane
Newtown
NT6 5NL

Date	Item	Debit	Credit	Balance
10. 11. 0–	Inv. 32781	£382.90		£382.90
16. 11. 0–	Inv. 34288	£ 96.54		?
23. 11. 0–	Credit Note 454		£23.45	?
28. 11. 0–	Inv. 38277	£176.23		?
			Amount Due	£632.22

Task 13.6

A statement of account has been received from the book supplier (see above). Copy the statement of account and complete the gaps by calculating how much the school owes the book publishers.

8 Remittance advice and cheque

The buyer will check the statement of account but if he/she does not want to pay the whole amount they will include a remittance advice with their cheque. This shows how much they are paying and which invoices their cheque is covering.

If all is in order and they want to settle the statement of account in full, a cheque is sent by the buyer to the seller for the amount of the total balance.

If payment is delayed beyond the period for which the cash discount is allowed, the amount owing will have to be paid in full.

Once the seller has received the cheque they will pay it into their bank account using a **paying-in slip**.

The seller may send a receipt showing how much has been received, however, this is only usually done when a cash transaction has taken place.

ELECTRONIC DATA INTERCHANGE (EDI)

– see Unit 12 Payment Systems

This is a system where all the business documents used in a transaction are produced on computers and sent between the buyer and seller via computer. No paper is involved.

Most businesses buy goods or pay for services on credit and use computers to keep a record of these transactions and send documents automatically to their customers. This saves labour time, reduces paperwork and the need for filing and therefore reduces costs.

Revision Questions

1 To obtain stock from a supplier, Louisa Designs would use ....

    an order form   an invoice   a dispatch note   a statement of account

2 When customers pay for a new dress, Louisa Designs gives them a
....

    receipt   order form   cheque   remittance advice

3 Fuller & Brandon's clients pay a deposit when buying a house. They usually pay this by
....

    cheque   invoice   receipt   credit note

4 The Fuller & Brandon accountant takes money to the bank once a week. He completes a
....

    statement of   invoice   delivery note   paying-in slip
    account

5 When the Finance Director of Nocha Ltd pays a supplier, he will request
.... as proof of payment.

    a cheque   a receipt   an order   an invoice

6 Once a month, Nocha Ltd receives from all its suppliers a record of financial transactions with them. This is called ....

    a statement of   a contract of   an invoice   a delivery note
    account   employment

7 When bears are received at 'Teddies on the Circle', they are checked against a
....

    receipt   cheque   credit note   delivery note

8 A document recording an increase in the price shown on an invoice is a ....

    credit note   delivery note   debit note   paying-in slip

9 A request for payment recording the details of the transaction is ....

    an invoice   a cheque   an order   a statement of account

10 A delivery note provides ....

    proof of   proof of   credit   debit
    purchase   delivery

Task 13.7

1   In small groups try to collect examples of the business documents mentioned in this unit:

a) order
b) delivery note
c) invoice
d) credit note
e) statement of account
f) remittance advice
g) cheque

2   Produce a wall chart that illustrates the process of a typical business transaction.

3   Using suitable software, design and create a set of documents, based on the documents you have collected. Include a logo and all the information you think necessary.

Task 13.8

It is important that Happy Ideas Ltd keeps accurate records of the goods it buys and sells.

1   The following are business documents. Select the FOUR used in the purchasing process and list them in the correct sequence.

cheque   credit note   invoice   order
paying-in slip   receipt   remittance advice   (4 marks)

2   Explain why receipts are important to customers of Happy Ideas Ltd. (2 marks)

3   What is the purpose of a cheque? (2 marks)

4   What would be the effects on Happy Ideas Ltd if cheques were received that contained errors? (2 marks)

(Edexcel, 2000 – F and H)

Extension task

1   K Marrs and Co supply lace to Louisa Designs. The contact details for both organisations are as follows:

K Marrs and Co
112 Sevenoaks Drive
Hastings Hill
Easington
DH1 4PL
Tel: 0191 5347692
Fax: 0191 5499001

Louisa Designs
23 The Hyde
West Taplow
Hertfordshire
EN7 8UF
Tel: 01587 287322
Fax: 01587 362436

Use suitable software to prepare an invoice from K Marrs and Co to Louisa Designs for the supply of:

100m of 25mm cream lace at £2.52 per metre
50m of white lace at £3.05 per metre
50m of satin trim at £2.30 per metre

Include a carriage charge of £4.50. Add VAT at 17.5%. Terms of sale 2.5% discount on 7 days.   (8 marks)

2   Explain why it is important to have a standardised procedure of financial recording.   (4 marks)

3   The following are documents used in business. Explain the purpose of each one.

a) credit note
b) quotation
c) statement of account
d) delivery note   (8 marks)

(Edexcel, 1996 – H)

MONEY TRANSFER SYSTEMS

WAGES AND SALARIES

> **At the end of this unit you should understand:**
> ▶ the different ways in which employees are paid
> ▶ how this pay is calculated
> ▶ how to read a pay slip
> ▶ how payments are transferred from employers to employees.

One of the most important reasons for working is the pay an employee receives for their labour. Employees are either paid in wages or salaries. Wages are paid weekly. Salaries are paid monthly.

HOW ARE EMPLOYEES PAID?

Wages

Most manual workers are paid weekly wages. The sum paid for a normal working week is known as the basic wage, for example, a machine operator earning £5.00 per hour for a 35-hour week will receive a weekly wage of £175.00, which is his/her basic wage. An employee's pay can be calculated in one of the following ways:

- time rate
- piece rate.

Time rate

In this method workers are paid for a set number of hours at a set rate, for example, £4.00 per hour for a 30-hour week. This time rate is usually agreed once a year between employers and trade unions or staff associations.

The actual rate set will depend upon the strength of the trade union and the demand and supply for a certain type of worker. For example, if anyone with few qualifications can do the job the rate will be low, if the job requires a number of qualifications and skills the rate will be high.

A firm may pay someone for a basic 30-hour week at £4.00 per hour. If the worker works more hours, say 33 hours, they are paid **overtime** for the three extra hours.

Overtime rates are usually paid at what we call **time and a half**. This means the worker in this case would receive £4.00 plus another £2.00 per hour, making a total of £6.00 per hour or £18.00 for the extra three hours.

They could also be paid what we call **double time**. This means receiving £8.00 per hour giving a total of £24.00 for the three hours.

Sometimes, employers will give workers time off work equal to the amount of overtime they have worked, instead of paying them. This is known as **time off in lieu**.

No. 501					Clock Card
Name: A Hannant					
Week ending: 6 April 2001					
Day	In	Out	In	Out	Total Hours
M	0800	1230	1330	1700	8
T	0800	1230	1330	1700	8
W	0750	1230	1330	1700	8
T	0800	1230	1330	1800	9
F	0800	1230	1330	1800	9
					42

Businesses that pay their workers by a time rate system must have a method of recording the hours worked by their employees. This may involve a clocking in system where workers clock in and out on a time-keeping machine so a record of their hours worked can be kept.

Many businesses now use a computerised system where workers use an electronic swipe card to clock in and out, which means that wages can be automatically calculated at the end of the week.

This system of payment is simple and cheap to operate. However, there is no real financial incentive for workers to work more quickly or to a higher quality, as they are guaranteed a set wage no matter how much they produce or what the quality is like.

Task 14.1

Copy out the table below and calculate how much overtime payment each worker has earned.

NAME	HOURLY RATE	HOURS OF OVERTIME	OVERTIME RATE	TOTAL OVERTIME PAYMENT
Jim Murray	£4.00	4	Double time	
Dave Fairclough	£4.00	5	Time & half	
Alison Armbrister	£5.00	10	Time & quarter	
Steve Huckle	£4.50	6	Time & half	
John Clements	£6.00	8	Double time	
Afroza Begum	£5.50	3	Time & half	

Piece rate

This is a payment system where the worker is paid for each piece of work they complete that meets a given quality standard. It is a common method of payment in the textile and electronics industries. For example, a worker in the electronics industry will be paid for each circuit board they complete to an acceptable standard.

This system encourages workers to produce as much as possible in the time available, which overcomes the problems of the time rate system. However, to ensure that low-quality goods are not produced, each worker's output has to be monitored closely so careful inspection is required.

Task 14.2

Anne Mills works in a clothing factory making jeans. She is paid £1.00 for each pair of jeans she makes. Once she has produced more than 200 pairs of jeans per week, the piece rate goes up to £1.50 a pair.

1 In a good week Anne can produce 250 pairs of jeans. Calculate her pay for that week.   (2 marks).

2 Some weeks Anne does not produce as many jeans. Suggest reasons as to why this might happen.   (6 marks)

3 What problems might there be if Anne tries to make up her lost production?   (4 marks)

Salaries

White collar workers are workers not involved in manual work and they are paid an annual salary. This salary is divided into twelve equal parts and paid each month into the employee's bank account. For example, an office worker earning £12,000 per annum will receive £1,000 a month.

A salary is paid either by cheque or electronically. The amount paid each month rarely varies as these workers are not usually paid for any overtime or extra work they do over and above their normal working hours. However, their pay may be increased through commission, bonuses or profit-sharing, which we will discuss later.

Salaried workers may also be on an incremental pay scale. This is a pay scale that increases each year. There will be a minimum and maximum rate of pay for the job. For example, the teachers' incremental pay scale is based on a nine-point scale, which ranges from £15–£24,000. This means that a new teacher will receive £15,000 per annum and will get an automatic pay rise each year until they reach the top of the pay scale.

Many public sector employees, such as nurses, the police and the civil service, are on such a pay scale.

In the private sector some employees' pay is decided between managers and unions or staff associations. Some of these jobs may also be on an incremental pay scale. The disadvantage of this system for employers is that employees get a pay increase each year irrespective of how good they are at their job. In addition, when an employee reaches the top of the scale they may become less motivated.

To overcome this problem many businesses have introduced performance-related pay. In this system, employees only get a pay increase if they achieve targets that have been previously agreed between themselves and their line manager or boss.

Additional payments

There may be other opportunities for earning more than the basic pay. Some of these are:

Commission

This is a payment system based on how much an employee sells. The amount of commission is worked out as a percentage of the amount sold. For example, an insurance salesperson may sell £1,000 worth of insurance and receive a commission of 10%. This means that the salesperson has earned £100.

Commission payments are usually paid to people who are employed in selling the products or services of a business. This system ensures that employees have to work hard to earn their pay but if they are successful their earnings can be unlimited.

Bonus

A bonus can be paid within both the time rate and piece rate systems. In the piece rate system, once a worker has produced more than their target levels, they will receive a payment greater than the basic piece rate for any items they produce. This encourages the worker to produce more.

Under the time rate system, a bonus is paid if the workers reach their production targets, which could be hourly, daily or weekly targets. This is to encourage workers to work at their maximum output and so overcome the problem of lack of incentive.

Profit-sharing

Profit-sharing is a system where businesses set aside a portion of their profits, which is then shared between their employees. It is usually paid as a bonus in addition to the employee's usual wage or salary.

Fringe benefits

Many workers today receive benefits other than pay from their employers. These benefits or 'perks' for manual workers include such things as a free uniform, discounts on products produced by the business, subsidised works canteen, free sports facilities and private healthcare.

Fringe benefits for non-manual jobs may include a company car, private healthcare, foreign holidays, private school fees paid and house-moving expenses.

Generally, the more important you are in the business, the more fringe benefits you receive. These have the added benefit of being tax free or taxed at a reduced rate.

Pay As You Earn (PAYE)

Unfortunately, an employee does not receive all the money they have earned (**gross pay**). They have to pay **statutory deductions**, which are income tax and national insurance contributions. This means that the employer is required by law to deduct these from the employee's pay. The amount the employee receives is their net pay.

Income tax

This is payable, subject to allowances, on all income that comes from being employed. The Inland Revenue is the government department responsible for collecting income tax.

Income tax is collected under a system known as Pay As You Earn (PAYE). Under this system, it is the employer's responsibility to deduct the correct amount from an employee's pay before he or she receives it. The tax is paid by the employer to the Collector of Taxes. This means that an employee pays their tax either weekly or monthly and not in a lump sum at the end of each tax year.

Employees have to fill in a tax form, which informs the Inland Revenue of all their earnings and expenses. From this information the Inland Revenue can calculate how much tax an employee should be paying. The amount of tax an employee pays will depend upon their income and which allowances they can claim. A personal allowance is the amount you are allowed to earn before you start to pay tax. These are some personal allowances:

■ a single person's allowance

■ a dependent relative's allowance

■ professional subscriptions (memberships fees if you are in a trade union).

Based on their personal allowances, a tax code is given to an employee by the Inland Revenue.

In order to calculate the tax payable, two books – Free Pay Tables (Table A) and Taxable Pay Tables (Tables B to D) – are used. These tables make it possible to see at a glance the tax due on any sum of money earned, according to an employee's tax code. Columns 1 and 2 show the highest amount of total taxable pay for which each table can be used for the week shown.

The amount of allowances determines the amount of tax-free pay – pay on which no tax is payable. Table A shows, for each tax code, the amount that can be earned before tax has to be paid. Table B shows tax due on the remainder of pay to date. Table SR shows the starting rate.

An employer has to record the pay records of all employees and how much tax is deducted from gross pay.

At the end of each year, an employee will receive a P60 form, which shows the total earnings for the year and the amount of tax deducted. When an employee leaves a job, they will receive a P45 form from their employer, which they have to give to their new employer so that they continue to pay tax without any complications.

Week	Column 1 Use Table SR on page 5 (£)	Column 2 Use Tables B on pages 8 & 9 (£)
1	29	539
2	58	1077
3	87	1616
4	116	2154
5	145	2693
6	174	3231
7	202	3770
8	231	4308

9	260	4847
10	289	5385
11	318	5924
12	347	6462
13	375	7000
14	404	7539
15	433	8077
16	462	8616
17	491	9154
18	520	9693
19	549	10231
20	577	10770
21	606	11308
22	635	11847
23	664	12385
24	693	12924
25	722	13462
26	750	14000
27	779	14539
28	808	15077
29	837	15616
30	866	16154
31	895	16693
32	924	17231
33	952	17770
34	981	18308
35	1010	18847
36	1039	19385
37	1068	19924
38	1097	20462
39	1125	21000
40	1154	21539
41	1183	22077
42	1212	22616
43	1241	23154
44	1270	23693
45	1299	24231
46	1327	24770
47	1356	25308
48	1385	25847
49	1414	26385
50	1443	26924
51	1472	27462
52	1500	28000

Table B

National Insurance

This scheme provides benefits for a variety of circumstances, for example:

- unemployment benefit
- Jobseeker's allowance
- income support
- incapacity benefit
- retirement pension.

In order to provide these benefits, people who work are required to pay National Insurance contributions. When you start work you will pay National Insurance contributions.

These contributions are related to your earnings and are assessed as a percentage of your gross pay. Contributions are shared between your employer and you, and are collected along with income tax under the PAYE process.

Income tax and National Insurance contributions are calculated each week or month and deducted from your earnings, which then gives your total net pay for the week or month.

Task 14.3

Amy Stenton works for an advertising agency. Her gross salary is £16,500. She has £320.50 deducted from her pay each month.

1 Calculate her monthly salary before deductions.

2 Calculate what her monthly take-home pay (net pay) will be.

The pay slip

A pay slip may take many forms and vary from employer to employer but it should contain the following basic items:

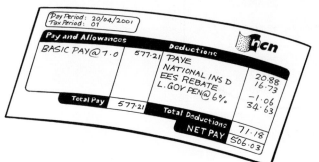

- basic pay – the sum paid for a normal working week without any additional payments like overtime

- gross pay – the total amount of money earned including any additional payments, eg overtime and bonuses, but before any deductions have been taken off

- overtime – the amount paid for any hours worked over and above the normal working week

- deductions – the money that is deducted from pay either statutorily (which means by law), eg income tax and national insurance contributions, or voluntarily (which means you choose to have them deducted), eg payments to a private pension scheme, savings or union fees

- tax code – the amount you are allowed to earn before paying tax eg 469L

- net pay – is the total amount of pay an employee receives after **all** deductions have been taken away from their gross pay ie their **take-home pay** or **net pay**.

Task 14.4

ORB Electricals				Pay Advice	
Payments			Deductions		
Basic Pay	40 Hrs	160.00	Income Tax		38.56
Overtime	10 Hrs	80.00	National Insurance		15.78
Bonus		15.00	Union Subs		0.50
			Total Deductions		?
Gross Pay		?	Net Pay		?
Gross pay to date		1678.00	Income Tax to date		380.79
Taxable pay to date		789.00	National Insurance to date		115.45

Date	Employee's name	Tax code	Tax period
23 August 2001	T.J. Smith	344L	6

Above is an example of a typical pay slip. Study the pay slip and answer the following questions:

1 What is the tax code?
2 What is the normal hourly rate of pay?
3 What is the rate of pay for working overtime?
4 What is the gross pay?
5 What are the total deductions?
6 What is the net wage?

Pay transfer

Once wages and salaries have been calculated by an employer, they can be transferred to an employee in three ways:

- cash

- cheque

- Bankers Automated Clearing System – BACS.

If an employee is paid in cash, he or she will receive a pay or wage packet. It is important that they check the money in the pay packet is correct before opening it. Most pay packets are designed so that the contents can be checked and any mistakes should be brought to the attention of the pay office immediately.

Although some manual workers are still paid in cash, many employers prefer to pay employees by cheque or BACS. This reduces the risk of wage robberies and the loss or theft of the employees' pay packets.

Employees can either write out individual cheques or, more increasingly, have them printed out by computer. The employer places the cheque in the pay packet with the payslip and gives it to the employee who can then pay the cheque into their bank or building society account.

Instead of using the above two methods, many employers are now transferring employees' pay directly into their bank or building society accounts. Employers have the bank or building society details of their employees and, through their own bank using a system known as BACS (see Unit 12 – Payment Systems), they are able to transfer pay to their employees.

The use of computers means businesses can quickly and accurately calculate pay, print pay slips, print details on cheques and transfer the amount of an employee's pay from the employer's bank account to the account of the employee.

Work patterns

Not everybody works the usual hours of 9.00 am to 5.30 pm. Some jobs are needed 24 hours a day, seven days a week, 365 days a year, for example, the emergency services of the police, fire and ambulance. Consequently, work patterns have to be arranged to cover all this time, for example, shift work and flexitime.

Shift work

In manufacturing industries, to make sure that machinery is working all the time and to make it more cost effective to run, a shift system may operate. This means that one set of workers starts work as the other set of workers finishes.

The shift system may involve:

- a day and night shift
- a three-shift system of eight hours each shift
- two weeks on and two weeks off.

An extra allowance may be paid to employees because of the unsociable hours they have to work.

You may know someone who works a shift system. Discuss with the rest of your class what type of work these workers do. Can you think of other jobs that involve working a shift system?

Flexitime

In today's increasingly busy society, many employees find it difficult to work the regular hours of nine to five due to their personal commitments. In the modern workplace, flexitime is being used more and more. This is where employees choose the hours that they work, which best fit in with the demands of their personal lives. They agree to work a core time, usually between 10.30am and 3.00pm but may choose when they work the rest of their hours provided they work the minimum number of hours per week or month.

Do you know of anyone who works flexitime? Ask them how it suits them.

Revision Questions

1 When employees receive a wage they are paid ....

   weekly   monthly   annually   daily

2 If an office worker receives an annual salary of £24,000 a year, what is their gross monthly salary?

   £12,000   £2,000   £1,000   £6,000

3 A system that lets workers choose their working hours is ....

   overtime   flexitime   full-time   a 3-shift system

4 If an employee works extra hours on top of their standard week, this is known as
   ....

   fringe benefits   bonus   overtime   commission

5 A payment system based on the hours worked is called ....

   piece rate   bonus   commission   time rate

6 Which of these is a fringe benefit for a non-manual worker?

   free uniform   subsidised canteen   company car   bus pass

7 Which of these is a statutory deduction from an employee's pay?

   income tax   union fees   private pension   savings

8 The money an employee receives, after all deductions have been taken off, is their
   ....

   gross pay   tax code   net pay   overtime

9 A form, which shows a summary of the tax paid by an employee at the end of the year, is a
   ....

   P45   P60   P2   P50

10 The system used to transfer an employee's pay automatically to their bank account, is known
   as ....

   electronic data   electronic point   tele-banking   bankers automated
   interchange   of sale   clearing system

Task 14.5

Explain the advantages and disadvantages, to employers and employees, of working flexitime and shift work.   (12 marks)

Task 14.6

The wages of production workers in Stoneybridge are calculated on an hourly rate.

The wages of outworkers are calculated on a piece rate.

1 State TWO differences between these methods of calculating pay. (2 marks)

2 Happy Ideas Ltd uses a spreadsheet for wage calculation and analysis. Below are the pay details for Martin Langford, a production worker.

Week 1	40 hours and 3 hours overtime	deductions of £121.62
Week 2	40 hours and 4 hours overtime	deductions of £117.60
Week 3	40 hours and no overtime	deductions of £91.65
Week 4	40 hours and 4 hours overtime	deductions of £101.45

Basic pay is £7.00 per hour and overtime is paid at time and a quarter. 1% of Martin's gross pay is deducted to pay his union subscriptions.

a Load the file WAGE (which your teacher will have already keyed in for you). Complete the data entry and calculate Martin Langford's pay for each week. (6 marks)

b Julia Clements wants a graph to show Martin's overtime pay for the last four weeks. Using appropriate software, prepare a graph to show this. (4 marks)

(Adapted from Edexcel 2000 – H)

Extension task

A new electronics factory, which makes silicon chips, is being built. The Managing Director has asked you to investigate the best method of paying the employees that will get them all working as a team, keep everyone happy and maximise production.

Prepare a short report for the Managing Director in which you will:

■ compare the strengths and weaknesses of the different methods of payment that could be used

■ recommend which method, or combination of methods, would be most suitable – give your reasons. (12 marks)

CONSTRAINTS AND INFLUENCES ON SYSTEMS

LEGISLATION

At the end of this unit you should understand:

▸ Data Protection

▸ Computer Misuse

▸ Copyright Designs and Patents

▸ Equal Opportunities.

DATA PROTECTION ACT

We expect 'the right to privacy'. We would therefore not expect personal details, such as our age, medical record, personal family details etc, to be available to anyone who wanted them. With technology advancing as fast as it is, there are many databases that hold very large amounts of information. Computers and networks are able to share this information rapidly around the world. So that there is some control over what is shared and distributed, as well as to protect people's right to privacy the Data Protection Act was introduced. The first Act became law in 1984.

However, the Act was updated on 16 July 1998 and now **regulates** the **processing** of information relating to individuals. This could include the obtaining of information, the holding or storing of information or the **disclosure** of such information.

Data could mean a variety of things but the Act mainly concerns itself with the following:

■ data which is intended to be used on a computer or other such equipment

- data that is recorded with the intention that it is going to be used by a computer for recording purposes

- data that is recorded as part of a filing system.

The Data Protection Act is constantly being updated to take into account all the changes that occur in our society with regard to how information is stored. The Internet and loyalty cards etc use huge customer databases for marketing purposes. The updated Act now covers manually held data, which the previous Act did not cover.

There is now a great deal of responsibility on the people that record and process personal data. They are known in the Act as **Data Controllers** and they must be totally truthful about the reason they are collecting the data and how they are going to use it. They must also inform the **Data Protection Commissioner** (this is the person who enforces the Act). One of the other things that they must do is to follow the rules and regulations laid down by the Act. Failure to follow the procedures could cause problems for the company they are employed by (as detailed later on).

The details of the Act are extremely complicated because they are not written in everyday English. They are written in a format that is acceptable in the courts and for Parliament to pass them as rules and regulations, which the Queen has to put her official stamp of approval on. The following points are included:

1 Any personal data must be processed correctly and follow the strict guidelines laid down. In particular, it should not be processed unless at least one of the following conditions are met:

   - the person whose data it is has given **permission** for the processing

   - the process is relevant for what the information is needed for

   - the Data Controller has the legal right to process the information or data

   - the processing is necessary to protect the interests of the person (eg a criminal court will not disclose the information about a person's conviction)

   - the process is necessary for the administration of justice or for a government department.

2 Personal data, ie marital status, salary etc, should only be obtained for one or more specific and lawful purposes and this information will not be further processed in any manner that **conflicts** with the original purpose.

3 Any personal data should be adequate, relevant and not be asking too much, in relation to the original reason the information was asked for and processed.

4 Personal information should be sufficient and if possible kept up to date where necessary.

5 Personal data that is processed for any reason or purpose should not be kept for any longer than is absolutely necessary.

6 Any personal data should be processed in accordance with the rights of the person under the regulations of the Act.

7 Every effort should be made to ensure that organisations take great care against anyone who is not **authorised** or illegally attempts to process the personal data, together with ensuring against accidental loss, destruction of or damage to the information collected.

8 The personal data should not be transferred to another country or area outside the European Economic Area, unless that country or territory has taken adequate precautions to protect the rights and freedom of the information in relation to the processing of personal data.

Sensitive personal data

The Act mentions data that is called sensitive personal data and some of this information may not be disclosed. For example:

1 racial or ethnic origin

2 membership or non-membership of a trade union

3 any proceedings for an offence committed or alleged to have been committed and, if convicted, the actual sentence

4 political opinions

5 religious beliefs

6 mental or physical welfare.

The Data Controller is really the person or group of people who actually make the decision as to what information is collected and what is done with the information.

Task 15.1

The above wording is very difficult to understand and quite often the words used are difficult to change into everyday language. Use a dictionary to look up all the words in bold plus any other words you are not familiar with.

Task 15.2

The information collected about pupils' eating habits is to be stored on the school's computer network. Some of the data kept on the computer about the pupils is personal information.

Explain why the Headteacher needs to be aware of the Data Protection Act. (3 marks)

(Edexcel IT, 1996 – H)

Data Subjects and Data Controllers

Everyone, whether we like it or not, is a 'data subject' because organisations and companies, called 'data users', hold personal details about us on their computer systems. What concerns everyone is that because of the power and the ease of communication between computers, a simple press of a button can transfer data from one computer to another. This means that data collected by one computer user can be transferred to other users, who can then use the information for a very different purpose.

The examples below are of information being transferred:

1   A television rented from a rental company – the rental company could transfer the information about you renting a TV to the TV Licensing Centre.

2   Another example could be your Driving Licence – details could be transferred to the Police National Computer along with details of the vehicle you own.

3 Unfortunately, we have no choice on our banks and building societies – they automatically inform the Inland Revenue if we receive interest above a certain amount.

However, the transfer of information from one computer to another does have certain advantages. For example, if the information of criminals was not transferred quickly from one police station to another in perhaps another part of the country it could mean that we might not be able to catch as many criminals.

There are, however, many dangers in information changing from one computer to another. What happens if the information or records get mixed up with someone else's or the information that is entered into the record is not correct? This could cause many problems:

■ You could be accused of a crime you did not commit.

■ You could find yourself driving a car that was yours but that had been reported stolen.

■ You could be accused of taking more money out of your bank account than was legally yours.

A more typical example is that you get refused a credit card or a loan because the records held on you are incorrect.

The Data Protection Act gives you the right to see the personal data kept on computer and if it is incorrect to get it corrected. We also have the right to complain to the Data Protection Registrar if we do not like the way the data was collected or the way in which it is being used.

Does everyone have to register if they keep any data for personal use?

No, not everyone has to register their use of personal data, so if you hold your address book, birthday list or Christmas card list on your home computer you do not need to worry.

There are exemptions to the use of personal data. If you believe that the data held falls into any of the categories overleaf then it does not have to be registered:

■ used only in connection with personal, family or household affairs or for recreational use

■ used only for preparing text for documents

■ used only for the calculation of wages and pensions or for the production of accounts

- used for the distribution of articles or information (eg unsolicited mail – commonly known as 'junk mail' – mail that you have not requested or asked for)

- held by a sports club or a recreational club that is not a limited company.

Do I have rights as a Data Subject?

Yes you do: you have the right to see any personal details held on computer about you or even held on manual records. You also have the right to a description of the data being processed. For example, if you do not understand what it actually means you can have it explained to you. You can see the details by sending a letter or e-mail to the company or organisation holding the data.

A typical letter is shown below.

Your name and address

Date

Dear Sir or Madam

I would be grateful if you could forward to me details of the information that you hold about me, which I am entitled to under the Data Protection Act 1998, or confirmation that no information is being held about me.

If you require further information or a fee, please let me know as soon as possible.

If you do not normally handle these requests for your organisation, please pass this letter to your Data Protection Officer or another appropriate official.

Yours faithfully

The company may ask for a small fee to cover the administration costs incurred in providing the information you requested. However, they must respond within 40 days of your request regardless of the charge of a fee.

There are, however, certain restrictions in that you do not have the right to see all the information held on you. You could be denied the information if it is being used for any of the following purposes:

- medical or social workers' reports

- collecting taxes or duty (eg VAT)

- catching or prosecuting offenders

- detection or prevention of crime.

Personal data that could form part of a confidential reference (application for employment or a college course etc) is also exempt from access. This means that you have no legal right to ask to see a confidential or personal reference about yourself.

Examination scripts and marks are also exempt from access. This means that you cannot demand to see your examination papers or the results before they are officially published. Some examination boards do return examination papers back to centres once the results have been published and any issues about grades awarded have been dealt with.

New symbol

The new symbol, a padlock which is open and has an 'i' on the lock part, is used to alert people to the fact that their information is being collected. It directs them to sources that will clearly explain how their information is to be used.

Look out for the symbol when you are giving your personal information out.

Task 15.3

Fred is aware that the information he has given to Gig Promotions could be used by that company for reasons other than issuing tickets.

The Data Protection Act protects the rights of people with regard to the use of personal information held on computer systems.

1 Explain fully what rights this law gives Fred to see and to change information on the Gig Promotions computer system. (4 marks)

2 Describe ONE legal use of the information about Fred.

(2 marks)

3 Describe ONE illegal use of the information about Fred.

(2 marks)

4 Describe ONE other way Fred might want Gig Promotions to use his information. (2 marks)

(Edexcel IT, 1999 – H)

Task 15.4

Polly is aware that the information she has given to O-zone could be used for reasons other than issuing tickets.

She does not want this to happen.

1. Describe ONE other way that O-zone might use the information about Polly to help their business. (2 marks)

2. Give ONE way Polly might NOT want her information used. (2 marks)

The law protects the rights of people with regard to the use of personal information held on computer systems.

3. State the name of the law that does this. (1 mark)

4. Explain how Polly could use this law to limit the way O-zone uses her personal information. (3 marks)

(Edexcel IT, 1998 – F)

COMPUTER MISUSE ACT

The Computer Misuse Act 1990 states that it is illegal to obtain authorised access to any computer or to modify its contents. There are three criminal offences, which are defined in this Act, namely:

- unauthorised access to computer material
- unauthorised access with intent to commit or help in further offences
- unauthorised modification of computer material.

It should be realised that this Act applies to all computers not just central services but covers workstations and PCs.

With the continuing growing use of computers and communication systems there were many problems that began to arise to do with the misuse of systems. The problems mainly concerned the variety of uses not covered by laws that already existed. Numerous cases were brought before the law courts but unfortunately they were unable to convict because the older laws did not cover the misuse.

Such cases were when people were able to 'hack' into other people's computers and read their mail, personal finances and anything else they had saved on their computer. Some clever computer users were 'hacking' into large companies' computer systems and then selling on the information they gained. The courts were unable to convict them on charges of theft – because as such they had not actually taken anything. They advised Parliament that new laws regarding this misuse of information were needed so that people could be prosecuted if they actually broke the law and gained access in this way to information that was not rightfully theirs.

This gave rise to the Computer Misuse Act 1990.

The Computer Misuse Act 1990 covers a variety of misuses, which were not covered by existing laws. It deals with the following:

- deliberately planting viruses into a computer system to cause damage to program files and data

- using computer time to carry out unauthorised work, such as using a firm's computer to run a friend's business

- copying computer programs illegally (ie software piracy)

- hacking into someone's system in order to see all the information or even change some of the information

- using a computer for various frauds; people have been known to put fictitious employees on a payroll program and use false bank accounts opened in the name of these employees to steal money. The film *Brewster's Millions* was a prime example.

Software piracy

Software piracy is concerned with illegally copying computer software. It is estimated to cost the software developers around £4000 million per year. It has been estimated that around 70% of the software used in Europe was illegal in the early 1990s.

If a company wished to design a computer program to use within their company it would take them many many hours of hard work, writing the program, testing the program, refining the program without taking into account the actual cost. This writing of programs does take place in many companies and usually there is a team of people working on the project. A rough estimate would be ten programmers spending 300 hours each writing the program. This equals 3000 hours at an estimated cost of £25 per hour giving a total of £75,000. Most companies would not be happy if they found out that someone had copied the program and was using it free of charge.

Elimination of unauthorised access

To avoid the piracy of software many companies will go to great lengths to ensure that access to their computers is as secure as possible. The simplest way is to allow only those who should have access to the computer, access. The next step is to give people a password that only they know. This password must then be keyed in. A password used to enter computer software will never appear on the screen, should always be changed regularly and should never be written down. Always try to avoid the obvious, such as surnames, Christian names etc. Many large companies use software to limit each user's access. For example, the access to software that a student might have will be different from that of a lecturer or teacher, or accounts clerks might only have access that allows them to do their job, but the accountant will have access to all financial accounts.

Another main factor when using computers in companies is that only a certain number of people have access to the computer's operating system. This is particularly important for those people who do not have much experience. A simple command at the operating systems prompt can delete an entire hard drive. Restricted access can also be used to prevent people from copying data from the hard disk to a floppy disk.

Viruses

Viruses are a type of program with the main purpose of disrupting the use of the computers. Some of the viruses do little more than display a message (these can sometimes be very abusive or even insulting!) on the screen. Others are designed to cause mayhem or confusion. Some have been known to wipe computers of all their software and therefore a person would have to re-install everything from scratch and rebuild the computer system. Some work after a period of time, such as after the millennium, or even make the letters on the screen start to fall away or drop down. As the name suggests they are spread by 'infecting' and they do this by copying themselves on to the computer. With the wide use of e-mail, the virus can spread across the world in seconds.

Viruses are quite common especially in situations where there are a large number of users, such as in a school or college. Today, most people install anti-virus software onto their machines. This will not stop those who send a virus by e-mail. Never open attachments on e-mail from people you do not know – it could be a virus!

Anti-virus software

Anti-virus software can be used to scan a computer's memory and disks to detect viruses. The software removes any viruses that are detected – this is similar to disinfecting a disk or cleaning. Be careful when choosing anti-virus software – speed is essential, therefore, do not buy a very slow one as you may not have the patience.

The following are helpful hints to avoid viruses:

- Do not buy second-hand software – unless you can scan it first.

- Check your computer for viruses on a regular basis or if you have had it repaired.

- Do not download software from bulletin boards, since this is the easiest way for the people who produce viruses to distribute their handiwork.

- Be careful of all software that is distributed freely, such as shareware, and software that comes free with a magazine, as these are susceptible to viruses.

- Try and avoid the changing of disks from one computer to another, as this tends to increase the possibility of gaining a virus.

- On your own machine install a reputable anti-virus software program and ensure that it is used regularly.

COPYRIGHT DESIGNS AND PATENTS ACT (1989)

The Copyright Designs and Patents Act makes it a criminal offence to copy or steal software.

Under this Act it is an offence to copy or distribute software or any part of the manuals that accompany it, without permission or a licence from the copyright owner. This person is normally the software developer.

You cannot run software on more than one machine unless you have purchased a licence that specifically allows it, for example, purchasing one copy of a program does not allow you to use it on a network. A special licence must be bought for the software to be used on the number of machines that you have on the network.

The Act does not allow you to copy the software or distribute it for use by an organisation. This means that you cannot copy the software and give out copies to everyone that works at a company.

EQUAL OPPORTUNITIES

A good employer will always treat employees fairly if he/she appreciates the importance of well-motivated staff. However, not all employers treat their employees fairly so there is legislation which sets out the rights and responsibilities of employers and employees.

To ensure all employees are treated fairly the Equal Opportunities Commission (EOC) was set up under the Sex Discrimination Act 1975 and has the authority to issue Codes of Practice which companies must follow. If they do not follow or fail to observe any part of the Act, then they could be liable for prosecution.

The EOC issues this Code of Practice for the following purposes:

- the elimination of discrimination in employment

- to give guidance as to what steps it is reasonable for employers to take to ensure that their employees do not in the course of their employment act unlawfully, contrary to the Sex Discrimination Act (SDA)

- the promotion of equality of opportunity between men and women in employment. The SDA prohibits discrimination against men, as well as against women. It also requires that married people should not be treated less favourably than single people of the same sex or vice versa.

More and more women are going out to work in Britain every year. The percentage of working women has risen rapidly over the last decade. It is estimated that by 2005 nearly three quarters of women will be working. This figure is at present lower than in other European countries. The main reason for this being that women who have children are now returning back to work and it is estimated that well over half of the women who have children under the age of five will return to work.

From statistics it is shown that girls are out-shining boys in examination results and more and more girls are obtaining higher qualifications. Yet even with the above figures women (who now make up approximately half of the workforce) do not receive equality with men. Despite the various Acts that were introduced, the Equal Pay Act of 1970 and the Sex Discrimination Act of 1975, women still have lower pay and less opportunities.

Opportunity 2000

Opportunity 2000 was set up in 1991 to encourage businesses to set targets for better opportunities for women, which could be achieved by the year 2000. About 300 businesses joined the campaign to increase women's success. There has been a marked increase in the number of women holding more senior posts. Companies are providing opportunities for women to return to work by job-share, longer maternity leave, career breaks, part-time work and even childcare support.

Equal Pay Act 1970

Female employees should be paid the same wage as male employees if they are doing the same work in terms of effort, skills and decision-making. The work does not have to be exactly the same but does need to be of equal value. For example, a cook in a small building business might expect to have equal pay to painters and plasterers employed by the business.

Sex Discrimination Act 1975

Female or male employees should not be at a disadvantage in their employment just because of their sex. For example, women should not be overlooked for promotion just because they are married and might start a family. This protection also applies to the recruitment process for jobs and other aspects of employment, like hours of working and dismissal.

Race Relations Act 1976

The Race Relations Act makes it illegal to treat a person less favourably than others on racial grounds. These cover grounds of race, colour, nationality (including citizenship) and national or ethnic origin. In practice, most racial discrimination in Britain is against people from ethnic minorities but everyone of every background, race, colour and nationality are protected by the law. If you think you have been discriminated against on racial grounds, the Act gives you the right to take your complaint before an employment tribunal or county court.

Task 15.5

When Jean Jones applied for a part-time job at a local solicitors, she thought she would stand a good chance of getting the job. Before having her two children she had worked for five years as a legal secretary. She also had excellent references. But despite being invited for interview, the job went to another candidate who was new to legal work. When she asked the head of the solicitors why she didn't get the job, she was told that they thought she would be unreliable. They thought the demands of her children would cause conflict between work and home life.

1 Make a list of the arguments that the employee might use.

2 Make a list of the arguments that the employer might use.

3 Give details of your reasons for the decision you finally make as to which party is acting correctly.

There is a great problem with laws because they can be very expensive for a small business to apply. There are many examples where employees in small organisations are not provided with all the legal rights they should have. It can also take an employee a long time to get a matter put right. In smaller companies, ie sole traders or partnerships, both sides rely a lot on each other behaving properly within the law. In larger organisations, which have Human Resources Departments and trade union representatives, it is easier to ensure that workers' rights are protected.

Revision Questions

1 Nocha Limited has .... policy to make sure that all employees are treated the same.

a Data Protection   a Quality Control   an Equal Opportunities   a Hardware and Software

2 Conditions for employees in the office of Harbon Estates Limited are subject to the
....

Consumer Credit Act   Data Protection Act   Sales of Goods Act   Health & Safety at Work Act

3 As employers, which of the following is a legal requirement for Harbon Estates Ltd?

A   Health and Safety
B   Work patterns
C   Access and location
D   Skills and training

4 The Information Technology Manager has written .... policy, which is hoped will inform employees of the hazards of using computers.

a Health and Safety   an Equal Opportunities   a Data Protection   an Equal Pay

5 Docdel Limited must abide by the Health & Safety at Work Act. This affects employees'
....

A   working conditions
B   wages and salaries
C   holidays
D   pensions

6 Louisa Designs has a policy where all employees are treated the same. This is known as
....

A   job evaluation
B   equal opportunities
C   collective bargaining
D   on-the-job training

7 Employees making bears at Happy Ideas Limited are protected by the
....

Consumer Protection Act   Health & Safety at Work Act   Sale of Goods Act   Trade Descriptions Act

Task 15.6

An extract from the Equal Opportunities policy of Harbon Estates Limited is given below:

'That no employee is treated differently because of sex, race, colour, ethnic origin, religion, disability or marital status . . .'

Explain TWO reasons why Harbon Estates Limited has an Equal Opportunity Policy. (4 marks)

(Edexcel, 1998 – F)

Task 15.7

Paul Kendall of Goodwin Limited needs a database of all employees.

Explain the importance of accuracy when entering employees' data, with reference to the Data Protection Act. (4 marks)

(Edexcel IT, 1995 – H)

Task 15.8

Docdel plc has an Equal Opportunities policy.

Explain how this might affect employees of Docdel Limited.
(3 marks)

(Edexcel, 1997 – H)

Extension task

The Directors of Nocha Limited have extended the duties of Laura Hughes to include the role of Equal Opportunities Officer. She will work for the Personnel Officer and be responsible for equal opportunities within the company.

1   Select TWO areas of concern she might discuss with the Personnel Officer regarding equal opportunities and give reasons for these concerns.   (8 marks)

The Directors of Nocha Limited have to ensure that the company complies with government legislation as follows:

  ● Computer Misuse Act 1990

  ● Data Protection Act 1998

2   Discuss the responsibilities the Directors have to their employees in relation to each Act. Consider the consequences to the directors if they fail in their responsibilities.   (12 marks)

(Edexcel, 1999 – H)

CONSTRAINTS AND INFLUENCES ON SYSTEMS

HEALTH AND SAFETY

At the end of this unit you should understand:

▸ the importance of a safe working environment

▸ the consequences of failure to comply with the relevant legislation.

HEALTH AND SAFETY AT WORK ACT (1974)

This Act sets out the duties and the responsibilites of employers and employees to ensure health and safety at work. It covers all places of work, such as offices, factories, farms, schools etc.

Employer duties and responsibilities

The law states that 'It is the duty of every employer, so far as is reasonably practicable, to ensure the health, safety and welfare at work of all his employees' (Health and Safety at Work Act S2.1). This means that every employer should study the conditions that the workforce operate under and ensure that they are as safe and healthy as is possible depending on the type of work involved.

Employers need to:

- provide a working environment for employees that is safe and without risks to health
- provide machinery and systems of work that are safe
- make sure that all entrances and exits are safe
- enforce safety standards and regulations
- investigate all accidents
- provide all necessary safety equipment and clothing free of charge
- provide information, instruction, training and supervision in the workplace.

It is also important that employers ensure that their employees know about any risks and hazards they may meet in their job and employers must:

- produce information in the form of a leaflet or poster about Health and Safety in their place of work
- produce a safety policy for their workplace and make sure that all employees are aware of the contents of the policy
- consult with representatives of the employees about matters related to Health and Safety. If there is a trade union representative at the workplace, he/she is allowed by right to inspect the working environment.

Employee responsibilities

Employees also have certain responsibilities when they are at work. They should:

- take reasonable care of their own Health and Safety and that of anyone else who may be affected by anything they do at work
- co-operate with their employer regarding any instructions or orders the employer gives about any Health and Safety matters
- protect themselves, for example, by wearing safety clothing and keeping work areas clear

■ not interfere with or misuse any equipment provided by the employer to make the workplace a safe and healthy environment for the workforce, for example, by not moving safety guards on machines

■ report any defects they find in machinery or work areas.

Task 16.1

Your school is having a new block of classrooms built. Make a list of all the Health and Safety risks that could arise on the building site.

COMPUTER HEALTH AND SAFETY

In this book, we are particularly concerned with the use of computers and so we will look at these in more detail.

Special guidelines have been produced on the safe use of VDUs in the Health and Safety (Display Screen Equipment) Regulations 1992. These regulations apply to staff who are classed as users of display screens and the equipment they use. Employers should:

■ look at each workstation (the desk, chair, VDU, keyboard and mouse) individually and make sure they are safe and comfortable for the users

■ provide eyesight tests and help with prescriptions if spectacles are needed as a result of VDU work

■ provide frequent breaks or changes in activity for VDU users

■ provide training and information for employees in the use of each piece of the workstation apparatus

■ provide screens that are adjustable so that they tilt and swivel, chairs that are adjustable in height with a tilting backrest and which swivel on a five point base and keyboards that are separate and moveable.

OTHER RELEVANT LEGISLATION

Apart from the Health and Safety at Work 1974 and the Health and Safety (Display Screen Equipment) Regulations 1992, other recent laws and regulations that protect the Health and Safety of workers are:

Working Time Regulations 1998

These provide new rights for workers regarding the right to:

- at least four weeks' annual paid leave

- eleven hours' consecutive rest in any twenty-four hours

- a day's rest per week

- a twenty-minute rest break after six hours work

- a limit of an average forty-eight hours in a week that a worker can be required to work.

These regulations were based on the view that excessive work is bad for employees' health.

Reporting of Injuries, Diseases and Dangerous Occurrences Regulations 1995

Under this Act, all employers or anyone in control of work premises is legally required to report work-related accidents or ill-health caused by work conditions and any dangerous occurrences.

This means that every workplace must have an Accident Report Book, which has to be completed with all the details of any accident that occurs, however minor. Details will include the name and job of the victim, the time, place and type of injury, as well as a full description of how the accident happened.

Employer's Liability (Compulsory Insurance) Act 1982

This means that every employer in the UK must be insured against any injury to an employee during the course of his or her employment.

Health and Safety (First Aid) Regulations (1981)

This lays down three broad duties:

- the duty of the employer to provide first aid

- the duty of the employer to inform employees of the arrangements for first aid

- the duty of the self-employed to provide first aid equipment.

This means that an employer should make an assessment of the first aid needs of their particular workplace taking into account the types of risks possible and the number of people employed. It is then the employer's responsibility to arrange first aid training for a number of members of staff and to ensure that first aid equipment is available.

FAILURE TO COMPLY

To ensure that these laws and regulations are carried out, a government-funded organisation called the Health and Safety Executive is responsible for appointing inspectors to carry out regular checks of work premises. The inspectors have the right of entry to workplaces without warning. This may be to investigate an accident or complaint or simply to make a general inspection and they can ban the use of dangerous machines or even close down the workplace if it is found to be unsafe.

If an employee is injured as a result of an accident at work, they may have a claim against their employer as long as they show that the employer's actions or inactions caused the injury.

Compensation may be claimed for the following, if they occur as a result of the accident:

- pain and suffering

- inability to do certain things, such as play sport

- loss of earnings

- expenses incurred

- the cost of any care that is needed.

Task 16.2

Study your school's Health and Safety Policy and answer the following questions:

1 Who is the person with overall responsibility for Health and Safety?

2 Who are the safety representatives?

3 Who are those trained in first aid?

4 How should an accident be reported?

Personal effects on employees

As we have already seen, there are special guidelines on the safe use of VDUs. The risks to the health of anyone who uses a VDU frequently are being researched all the time and we will study these risks along with the precautions that can be taken to protect yourself when using computers.

The main effects on computer users that we will look at are:

■ RSI – Repetitive Strain Injury

■ eye strain from VDU use

■ bad posture

■ risk of an accident.

RSI – Repetitive Strain Injury

This is the name given to a number of disorders that can affect the hands, wrists, arms, shoulders or neck of computer operators. It is inflammation of the joints and is caused by making the same small movements over and over again. It can cause pain, numbness, swelling and the inability to lift and grip objects. In some cases, operators have become permanently disabled and have had to give up work.

To reduce the risk of RSI, employers should provide keyboards that:

■ have concave shaped keys – to reduce the chance of the operators' fingers slipping off them

■ are separate from the VDU so the user can adjust them to their own individual taste

■ lie flat or slope at an angle of about 10°.

To reduce the risk of RSI, computer operators (and this includes you) should:

■ make sure the desk and chair are at suitable heights

- sit at a comfortable distance from the keyboard

- make sure that lower arms are horizontal and wrists straight when using a keyboard or mouse

- use a wrist rest if necessary so that you do not rest your wrists on the edge of the keyboard or desk

- take frequent breaks to stretch your arms and fingers.

Eye strain from VDU use

Using a VDU for long periods at a time may affect a user's eyes and in some instances cause headaches.

To reduce the risk of eye strain, employers should ensure that:

- desks and VDUs are arranged to avoid glare or bright reflections on the screen

- desks are positioned so that the user is not looking at windows or lights

- window blinds or curtains are provided to cut out unwanted light

- the display is sharply focused and individual characters do not move or flicker

- free eye tests are arranged for employees who request them

- they pay for glasses if special ones are needed for VDU use

- they provide training to make sure that employees use their VDU safely.

To reduce the risk of eye strain, computer operators should:

- adjust the screen brightness and contrast to suit the lighting conditions in the room

- adjust the angle of the screen to your sitting height

- keep the screen clean

- use a document holder so that you do not have to lean over to read documents

- take a break for a couple of minutes every 20 to 30 minutes.

Posture

The way you sit when using a computer is very important. Sitting incorrectly or without the right support at a computer terminal for long periods of time can result in back, neck and upper arm injuries.

To reduce the risk of injuries, employers should:

- provide an adjustable chair, which allows the operator to adjust the height so it is correct for the keyboard on the desk

- provide an adjustable backrest on the chair which tilts to support the user

- provide a chair that swivels on a five point base

- provide a suitable footrest if required.

To reduce the risk of injuries, computer operators should:

- adjust the chair and VDU to find the most comfortable position to work in

- adjust the backrest of the chair so that it supports your lower back

- always sit well back in the chair with your feet flat on the floor or on a footrest

- not sit in the same position for long periods at a time

- take frequent short breaks rather than fewer long ones, preferably including some walking about.

Task 16.3

The diagram below shows an ideal situation for a computer operator.

Make a copy of the diagram and label it to show the important points we have mentioned in the last three sections on RSI, eye strain and back injury.

Risk of accident

It is the responsibility of everyone in the workplace to help prevent accidents. Offices can be dangerous places unless people act with care and consideration for others.

It is important that employers make every effort to provide a safe workplace but it is also the responsibility of the employees to ensure that they do not undertake any activities that could cause accidents. They must always report any unsafe equipment as soon as it is noticed and any accidents, however slight, must be reported and entered into the official accident book, which is kept on all work premises.

Task 16.4

Many injuries at work are caused by people lifting even light items incorrectly. Find out the correct method to use for lifting any item. Design an eye-catching information sheet to be displayed in the workplace, advising employees how they should lift and move even small items so that they avoid injuries to their back, legs and arms.

Task 16.5

Find out and make a list of the Health and Safety regulations for working in a workshop or laboratory in your school.

Employer's decisions

Employers have to make important decisions about the equipment that is used in their workplace, the layout of the factory or office, the maintenance of the machinery or equipment and how their workforce is trained to use it.

If we take the example of a typical office, the employer would need to decide what hardware and furniture each employee requires and how the general layout of the room should be planned.

Many computer operators nowadays work at shaped modules called workstations, which provide a working and a keyboard area. Using a swivel chair allows both areas to be used easily. An example of a workstation is shown overleaf.

Employers also need to decide whether their offices are going to be open plan or cellular. Open plan means a large number of people working together in one big room, sometimes with screens between the workstations.

The advantages of an open-plan office are:

- communication between workers is quicker and easier
- managers and senior staff are able to supervise and keep in constant contact with the employees more easily
- more economical to heat and light.

The disadvantages are:

- little privacy
- security is much harder to maintain
- noisier
- workforce is much more likely to get distracted from their job.

Cellular offices are much smaller rooms usually for a maximum of four people.

The advantages are:

- greater security with a lockable door
- privacy
- quieter atmosphere to work in.

The disadvantages are:

- more expensive to maintain, eg cleaning a number of cellular offices takes much longer than an open-plan office
- time is wasted walking from office to office to communicate with other employees
- more expensive to heat and light.

Task 16.6

Imagine that you have been asked to design a cellular office for use by two people, the Marketing Manager and her personal assistant. Using the outline shown below, work out the best positions for the two people. Each one will need a workstation, chair and filing cabinet. In the room, they will also need one bookcase and one conference table with four chairs.

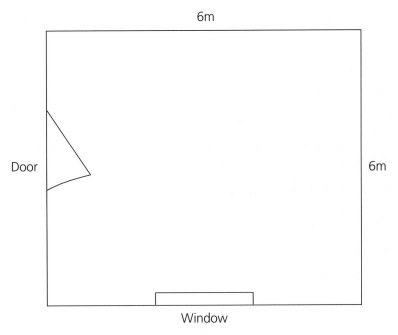

6m

Door

6m

Window

Training

The introduction of new technology into organisations makes it very important that staff should receive training to keep them up to date. They may need to learn new skills and techniques or upgrade existing ones.

Training can have a number of benefits.

For the workforce:

- They gain greater skills and knowledge.
- They have better career and promotion prospects.
- They are usually better motivated and more confident.

For the organisation:

- Employees are more efficient and better at their jobs.
- Employees are productive.
- They get better quality work.
- Employees take less time off work and stay longer in the organisation.

Training also has costs:

- It is expensive, especially training in the use of ICT equipment.
- It takes the employee away from their job and interrupts production.
- Output and quality may suffer during training.

Employers have to decide when training is necessary for their workforce and what type of training it will be.

Types of training

Induction training – this is for new staff. It introduces the new employee to the firm, the workplace and their fellow employees. It generally starts on the first day and includes information about the company and Health and Safety rules, as well as a tour of the site. It should help the new employee to feel welcome and enable them to settle into the routine of the firm more quickly.

On-the-job training – this is learning while working. It takes place within the firm and an experienced employee will show the trainee what to do and check their progress. This is relatively inexpensive and means that production is not interrupted but will probably be slowed down and the trainee may create a lot of waste.

Off-the-job training – this takes place away from the workplace and is conducted by specialist trainers and should therefore be of a high quality and up to date. It is more expensive than on-the-job training because the course has to be paid for and also the employee is not working productively while training. Many large companies have their own training centres, which are used by all their staff for every type of training from induction to retraining. Other companies use local colleges or specialist training companies. Off-the-job training often leads to some external qualification or award.

One other type of training, which is often used when staff need instruction in the use of computer systems, is to employ a specialist trainer to work with the employees in their own workplace. This is particularly useful in the case of a firm that has installed a new computer system, for example, as it means that employees are working at their own workstation, using familiar equipment, while receiving high-quality training. Although this type of training is expensive, it should enable the employees to acquire the necessary skills quickly and minimise the disruption to the company and its customers.

Revision Questions

1 The Health and Safety at Work Act (1974) sets out the .... and responsibilities of employers and employees to ensure health and safety at work.

duties   rights   wishes   orders

2 Employers need to provide information, instruction .... and supervision in the workplace.

schools   training   colleges   textbooks

3 Information in the form of a leaflet or .... should be produced to ensure that employees know about any risks or hazards in the workplace.

brochure   announcement   poster   television advert

4 Employees should report any .... they find in machinery or work areas?

people   defects   mistakes   extras

5 Working Time Regulations 1988 states that workers have a right to at least .... weeks' annual paid leave?

three   five   six   four

6 Every employer in the UK must be .... against injuries to their employees.

insured   taxed   outlawed   provided

7 Repetitive Strain Injury is caused by making the same .... movements over and over again.

circular   large   energetic   small

8 Employers should arrange for free .... tests for VDU operators who request them.

back   eye   neck   dental

9 Employers should provide .... chair for their employees, to reduce the risk of back injuries.

an arm   a relaxing   an adjustable   a dining

10 .... training is for new staff and introduces them to the firm.

off-the-job   on-the-job   induction   staff

Task 16.7

Full-time production workers employed by Happy Ideas Limited require training for the specialist work required or the production line. The three most common types of training are:

- induction
- on-the-job
- off-the-job

Select the most appropriate type of training for production workers and give reasons for your choice. (5 marks)

(Edexcel, 2000 – F)

Task 16.8

Employees working with computer equipment are protected under United Kingdom and European Union legislation. There are regulations covering the use of screens, safety of wiring and suitability of seating.

1 Explain how Docdel plc might meet their obligations under such legislation. (4 marks)

2 Explain the implications for employees if Docdel plc fails to meet its obligations under the legislation. (4 marks)

(Edexcel, 1997 – H)

Task 16.9

After induction, employees at Docdel plc receive on-the-job training. Explain TWO advantages to Docdel plc of charging to off-the-job training. (6 marks)

(Edexcel, 1997 – H)

Extension task

The directors of Nocha Ltd have to ensure that the company complies with government legislation as follows:

- Health and Safety at Work Act 1974

- Data Protection Act 1998

Discuss the responsibilities the directors have to their employees in relation to each Act. Consider the consequences to the directors if they fail in their responsibilities. (12 marks)

(Edexcel – 1999 – H)

Extension task

The introduction of information technology to Harbon Estates Limited is being planned by the Directors. The setting up of a network in their offices will raise a number of issues, which include Health and Safety.

Identify and give a detailed description of THREE different Health and Safety issues relating to the installation and use of computers at Harbon Estates Limited. (12 marks)

(Edexcel, 1998 – H)

CONSTRAINTS AND INFLUENCES ON SYSTEMS

SECURITY

At the end of this unit you should understand:

▸ the importance of security and confidentiality

▸ the consequences of a breach of security.

Every organisation needs to take security of hardware, software and data very seriously because the consequences of breaches of security can be extremely damaging to a business. They can mean loss of production, cash flow problems, loss of customers and reputation or even the eventual closure of the business.

Threats to security can be from outside (external) or inside (internal) the business and may be either accidental or deliberate.

SECURITY OF EQUIPMENT

First, we will look at the physical security of equipment – the computers and the other hardware, such as printers, scanners etc. What can be done to protect them from loss whether accidental or deliberate?

Accidental loss

Accidental loss is often concerned with portable laptop computers, which are genuinely misplaced. Laptop computers are small powerful computers that can be used anywhere and are very useful for people who need to be able to input information while on the move. An example might be a sales representative who visits many premises to gain orders for his/her company and needs to record the orders and download the information to their mainframe computer as soon as possible.

Because these machines are getting smaller and easier to carry, unfortunately, they are also easy to put down and forget. There is no real solution to this problem except to emphasise the need for continual care and vigilance by all personnel using laptops.

Deliberate theft

Protection against theft of computer equipment from offices and workplaces involves physical security. This means measures being taken to prevent unauthorised entry to a building or room, for example. Ways in which this can be done are, by:

- ensuring the whole building is secure and has an intruder alarm system and if necessary a closed circuit television system

- fitting metal bars or shutters on windows, particularly on the ground floor

- having a security alarm in IT rooms and a keypad lock on the door, which can only be opened by authorised personnel

- requiring all employees to wear an ID badge and all visitors to sign in and out and wear a temporary ID

- having security staff on duty twenty-four hours a day.

It is also important to protect the actual equipment from theft. This can be done by:

- using independent alarms on all hardware – these remain in operation when the main security alarms are inactive, for instance, during working hours

- attaching computers to desks using clamps etc

- always using the locks on computers and keyboards, if fitted, so that they cannot be turned on if they are stolen

- marking all equipment with ultra-violet pens and making a list of the serial numbers of the equipment so that if it is stolen and recovered, it can be traced back to its owner.

Task 17.1

Look at the ICT rooms in your school. See if you can identify the measures that are being taken to protect the computers and other hardware.

Task 17.2

Peter Evans is installing a local area network in his suite of four offices on a small business park. He only has a limited amount to spend on security for his computers and other hardware.

Look at the information above and, thinking about his circumstances, list the four most necessary security measures you think he should choose to install. Give reasons for each of your choices.

SECURITY OF DATA

Data is very valuable to an organisation and like computer hardware is at risk from accidental loss or deliberate damage and theft.

Accidental loss

This can be caused in a number of ways, such as:

- the document is accidentally deleted or unintentionally written over
- the computer breaks down or the power fails
- the file or disk becomes corrupted, for example, by scratches on the disk or a faulty disk drive
- the file is destroyed by fire or in a flood.

Back-up of data

(See Unit 4 Electronic)

We all know how infuriating it is to lose our work but loss of data can be as serious to a business as losing its stock. Therefore, it is very important to have more than one saved copy of all data by making a back-up copy, which can be used if anything happens to the working copy. This can either be done manually by creating a copy on some form of secondary storage or automatically by the computer.

- Secondary storage – a back-up copy of data is created on a secondary storage system, such as floppy disks, a CD-ROM or a magnetic tape streamer. All these involve transferring copies of data files onto another kind of medium so that they can be stored away from the original. They could be stored in another office, a fireproof safe or even in a building on another site.
- Automatic back-ups – computer programs give you the opportunity to create a back-up file, which you can recognise because it is given a name ending in

.bak. When you save a document, the old version is not lost, but renamed, so the old version of a file called EQUIPMENT.DOC would become EQUIPMENT.BAK and your new version would be EQUIPMENT.DOC. This is a useful replacement if for some reason you lose the current version of the file.

■ Another automatic back-up facility is when your program is set to do an automatic save every few minutes. This means that in the event of a power failure, you would only lose the work you have done since the last automatic save.

Task 17.3

Find out how the automatic save system works on your school or your home computer. Write down the answers to the following questions:

1 How do you alter the automatic save function on your word-processing program?

2 What are the most frequent saves it will do?

3 How do you know when it is doing a save?

4 What do you consider to be an appropriate time span between saves – give your reasons?

Deliberate damage

This is loss of data caused by viruses or hackers.

Viruses

(See Unit 15 Legislation)

A computer virus is a harmful program that copies itself onto your computer

and disrupts your work. Problems caused by viruses can range from irritating messages to deleting data or even erasing the entire contents of your hard disk. Viruses are transferred from one computer to another either by the use of infected floppy disks or over networks. They may work immediately or may be set to take action on a particular date; for example, the 'Friday 13th' virus is a well-known one.

Viruses cost businesses a great deal of money, both in repairing the damage they do to a computer system and in taking security precautions to try and avoid infection.

Although it is impossible to have a system that is not open to viruses – unless you use a stand-alone PC and never input data from disks or use the Internet – there are sensible measures that can be taken to reduce the risks.

- Use anti-virus software, which can detect and remove all **known** viruses. This needs to be updated regularly to account for newly developed viruses.

- Avoid using 'free' software, such as that distributed with magazines, unless you are sure about the origin.

- Write-protect all software programs so that viruses cannot change them.

- Make regular back-ups of files, so that if a virus does erase data, the files can be recovered.

- Never open a file attachment to an e-mail message from an unknown user – it could be a virus.

- Do not download software from bulletin boards unless you are confident about the origin.

- Make sure that all computer users are aware of the dangers of viruses.

Task 17.4

You are a systems manager in a large multinational company with branches worldwide. You receive information from Microsoft about a new, extremely dangerous virus. What actions should you take to try to prevent the virus affecting your system?

Hackers

A hacker is someone who gains unauthorised access to data held on a computer system. Hackers are often motivated by the challenge presented by security systems and their desire to 'hack' into them to see if it can be done. For example, there have been well-publicised cases of hackers who have penetrated the defence and national government systems of various countries.

However, many cases of hacking are for the purpose of committing fraud and are carried out either by employees of the company involved or by external hackers gaining access.

Although, as with viruses, no system is unbeatable against hackers, there are various ways to make hacking more difficult.

- Use passwords – these can be for the whole system and/or for individual users. A password has to be keyed in to gain access and is only known by authorised users. Passwords should be changed regularly.

- Restrict access to some data so that certain users do not have the right to see all the data held by an organisation.

- In the case of very sensitive data, introduce biometric methods of security, which identify authorised users by fingerprint, voice or face recognition.

- Encrypt files – this method is often used when sensitive data has to be transmitted from one part of an organisation to another. The data is 'scrambled' or coded before it is sent and then decoded when it is received at the other end. If the data is intercepted, it is unreadable to anyone who does not know the code.

- Set a limit on the number of times a user can attempt to enter a password, so that after, for example, three incorrect attempts, the user is disconnected.

Hacking and planting viruses are both criminal offences. There are severe penalties for anyone convicted under the Computer Misuse Act 1990. This Act is looked at in detail in Unit 15 Legislation.

Revision Questions

1 To provide a security watch on an organisation's premises, the company can install
....

ITV   microphones   CCTV   a digital camera

2 To prevent unauthorised entry to computer rooms a .... could be
fitted to the door?

Yale   keypad   mortice   padlock

3 Marking equipment with .... helps to trace stolen equipment back
to the owner?

an ultra-violet pen   a marker   an OHP   a biro

4 A back-up of data stored in a computer can be made using a ....
tape streamer.

floppy   magnetic   paper   disk

5 An automatic back-up file will have a name ending with ....

.com   .bak   .doc   .lwp

6 A harmful program that copies itself onto your computer without you intending it to is
....

an illness   a virus   a germ   a disease

7 To make sure that viruses cannot change them, all software programs should be
....

guarded   erased   write-protected   downloaded

8 One way to transmit viruses is by the use of floppy disks that are
....

second-hand   infected   used   spoiled

9 A hacker is someone who gains .... access to data held in a computer system.

authorised   official   unauthorised   unofficial

10 To protect sensitive data, files can be .... so that the data is scrambled and unreadable.

decoded   encrypted   entered   transmitted

Task 17.5

Before Peter Evans' LAN starts to operate, he tells all his employees that they must decide on a personal entry password so that they can gain access to the system. The password will have to be changed every two weeks.

1 Find out the advisory rules for creating passwords and make a list to advise the employees on choosing passwords and keeping them secure.

2 Why is it necessary to change the passwords every two weeks?

Task 17.6

Ask your family or friends who use computers at work the following questions.

1 Do they use passwords and how often are they changed?

2 What back-up systems are in place for the data in their organisations?

Extension task

1 Describe THREE ways data in a network system can be affected. How would you ensure the data was not affected?   (12 marks)

Extension task

1 You work for a company which holds customer records, financial records and employee records on a network. Describe how the company could ensure these records are not lost, accessed by unauthorised people or corrupted.

(12 marks)

CONSTRAINTS AND INFLUENCES ON SYSTEMS

OPERATIONAL

At the end of this unit you should understand how the efficient operation of systems can be affected by:

▸ effects on personnel

▸ work patterns

▸ equipment

▸ environmental issues

▸ market conditions.

In today's fast-moving society, we are constantly having to change, especially with regard to the jobs we have and the careers we pursue. Gone are the days when one would have a 'job for life'. Your grandparents probably started work for one company at the age of 15 or 16 and more than likely stayed with the same company until they retired. The majority of people tended to stay in one job – they may have progressed in the company but they would not consider changing their job unless forced to do so. Nowadays everything has changed. It is anticipated that in an average working life a person will not only change jobs several times but will also change direction in their career.

There is now no guaranteed 'job for life' so it is important to be prepared for change for a variety of reasons some of which are considered below.

EFFECTS ON PERSONNEL

Redundancy

Over the last 25–30 years there has been a gradual decline in the traditional industries that once made Britain one of the greatest industrial nations. Shipbuilding, steel-making and coal mining have almost ceased to exist in Britain, as low-cost countries have stepped in and eroded our once dominant position. Companies in these industries have closed or at best reduced in size as a means of survival. Employees of these companies have lost their jobs as their positions have become redundant. As a result of industries tending to congregate in a particular area of the country, such as shipbuilding in the north, coal mining in Wales and textiles in the Midlands, this has made finding another job more difficult as there were so many other people looking for work at the same time.

If a company makes its employees redundant, then it is obliged under Government Legislation to pay compensation dependent upon the length of service that a person has worked. Some companies pay the minimum amount of redundancy as stated in the legislation, while others are more generous and add to the compensation package. The money is considered to be compensation for the fact that the person is no longer employed. In the majority of cases, redundancy pay does not last very long because household bills for maintaining a home still have to be paid. In the past, people who have been made redundant became stigmatised as poor workers and found it extremely difficult to find new employment. However, because of the large-scale reduction in industry and the vast numbers of redundancies, this stigma is no longer relevant and it is almost a fact of working life that at some point you will lose your job as a result of circumstances totally beyond your control.

Voluntary redundancy

This is when a company calls for employees willing to be made redundant from the company. Many people consider this option if they have long service and are nearing retirement and the package offered by the employer can sometimes prove more lucrative than remaining in employment.

During the 1980s and 1990s, large numbers of manual and skilled workers, as well as white collar workers (these are people who work in offices etc), were made redundant because the technological age was beginning to take over. Robots and computers took over tasks that were being performed by people and therefore fewer people were required by the company to continue its business.

Job change

As discussed, the change from manual work to computers carrying out tasks has had a big impact on the type of work people now do and the skills required. People are required to have wider ranging skills but not necessarily be experts in all that they do. Flexibility is essential to any job and the degree of flexibility required will continue to increase as automation/robots/computers dominate the workplace.

Task 18.1

Smith Brothers is a very traditional firm that makes garden furniture by hand. This furniture sells well locally and is always in demand. Over the last year, there has been an increase in the number of people buying garden furniture, especially of the wooden type. The brothers have a big decision to make, do they expand their business and create more jobs for people or modernise the company and bring in technology and let the computers make the furniture?

The proposal has created a hostile reaction from the workers.

List the reasons for and against Smith Brothers changing their method of production of garden furniture.

Resistance to change

People are normally resistant to change when they fear the unknown. This is especially true when people become older, as they become more set in their ways and change becomes daunting. A person who has trained to be a typist suddenly finds the threat of a computer very frightening. It is not that their skills are no longer needed, it is the fear of the unknown but also the fear of actually coping with the work and the new technology. The typist would probably prefer to stay with the typewriter and would put forward many arguments or pointers as reasons for not changing.

Training systems

The pace of change is phenomenal and will continue as technology becomes more dominant. In order to thrive and remain successful, it is imperative that companies continually train and educate their employees. Modern companies should, over a designated period of time, aim to ensure that all have skills matrices and, over a designated period of time, should aim to ensure that every employee has the skills required to perform a certain number of tasks.

However, training involves time and money, neither of which modern companies have an abundance of. It is therefore a balancing act to ensure that employees are trained with the resources available. Attitudes to training vary among companies. A larger progressive company will consider that much more training is essential for its employees, while a smaller company may have to limit the training it can provide.

The subject of training is very contentious and can lead to many arguments as to the type of training needed rather than the actual cost of training. What type of method should be used and who should do it would be key considerations.

> *'I don't like training because you are not treated the same'* –
> YP Trainee
>
> ### 'If you give someone too much training they will go off and get a better job' – *Employer*
>
> 'There is never enough opportunity to train people properly – we need more equipment and more staff' – *Teachers*
>
> *Very different opinions on training from different aspects of life.*

Training is needed to:

- introduce a new process or new equipment

- improve performance and efficiency

- train unskilled workers

- reduce the need for supervision

- provide greater opportunities for the staff.

Personal reasons for training may be to:

- gain promotion to another job

- gain more money – increase pay

- reduce the number of accidents – more competent at what you are doing should mean that you are less likely to make mistakes.

Task 18.2

You have been given the task of trying to change the attitude of the people that work with you, with regard to training as they feel it is not worth it. Give your reasons and examples as to why you think they should change their attitude.

Task 18.3

List the main methods of training you can think of. Give the advantages and disadvantages of each type.

Task 18.4

Each new employee at Louisa Designs – a clothing manufacturer – has induction training.

1 Explain TWO reasons why this is necessary.   (4 marks)

2 Explain THREE ways in which the introduction of information technology might affect employees at Louisa Designs.
                                                      (6 marks)

(Edexcel, 1996 – F)

De-motivation

De-motivation is a lack of inspiration or stimulation that can apply to both life and jobs. A de-motivated person is someone who has lost interest or 'switched off', for whatever reason. It could be that the job has become boring to them, there is nothing to challenge them or because the atmosphere of the company is not very good. There may be threats of closure or redundancies plus many more reasons as to why someone becomes demotivated.

Task 18.5

The Directors of a company called Nocha Limited – an ice cream making company – need a new sales force, which will sell directly to major UK supermarkets and freezer centres.

Outline and evaluate suitable approaches to:

■ training

■ motivating. (8 marks)

(adapted from Edexcel, 1999 – H)

Job security/insecurity

Job security is considered by many people to be very important. Security provides stability, and this can lead to high motivation. Most employees want the satisfaction of knowing that they will have a job to go to and receive an income to continue to support their lifestyle. Job security is particularly important to those people who have the responsibility of a family. They want to know that when they take out a loan for five years they will still have a job that will allow them to make the repayments. If you decided to purchase a home, then the mortgage company would want to know that you are working in a job that will enable you to make the payments and that you have been employed with the company for some time, normally around two years.

Today, many companies are unable to provide permanent contracts and, as such, employ people on temporary contracts. Temporary contracts enable employers to hire and fire to suit the business cycle. However, temporary contracts provide no long-term stability for employees and job security does not come into question.

Task 18.6

Delta Homes plc, a property developer, has a Personnel Department. Much of the work of this department involves recruiting construction workers on temporary contracts.

1 Explain ONE reason why Delta Homes plc employs workers on temporary contracts. (2 marks)

2 Explain TWO problems for Delta Homes plc that might arise from employing workers on temporary contracts. (6 marks)

Anxiety

Anxiety is a state of uneasiness and troubled mind. Anxiety can be caused by many events both in and out of the work environment. Anxious workers spend more time focusing on their problems than they do on the job and, as such, perform less than those who are not anxious. Anxious workers are expensive as they can make mistakes that can affect product quality and potentially the lives of those they work with because they are not fully concentrating on the task in hand.

Working conditions

More and more employees are becoming reliant upon computers to perform their daily routines. Many people have to sit and stare at a computer screen for hours upon end and operate a keyboard. This constant repetitive and tedious work can lead to many health problems, such as RSI (Repetitive Strain Injury) and eye strain. Working areas need to be ergonomically designed to accommodate safe working practices. It is an employer's duty to ensure that its employees are provided with the necessary equipment to reduce health hazards and industrial injuries – screen filters, chairs that have arms and can be adjusted for height, back rests, gel-filled wrist supports etc. (See Unit 16 Health and Safety)

WORK PATTERNS

Working from home (teleworking)

Computers and technology have allowed more and more people to work from home, thereby negating the need for people to travel to offices. Computers stationed at home anywhere in the country can be linked to a company and employers do not have to rely on local labour to fulfil the workforce. This has many implications for both the employer and the employee. It creates many opportunities for the employee to be flexible – working when they have the time – and available, for

example a mother with young children can work after normal office hours when the children are asleep in the evening. If the children are ill there is no need to get child-minders or to take time off work.

For the employer it has many advantages, such as the fact that they do not have to provide the employee with premises to work from, they only have to supply a computer and a computer link. The heating and lighting costs are reduced for the company, canteen facilities are not needed plus many other benefits. Employers can use labour in areas of high unemployment thereby reducing the salaries they pay.

Teleworking has major benefits upon the environment because less people travel to work and therefore there are less cars or public transport on the roads, thereby reducing the pollution into the atmosphere.

Task 18.7

An increasing number of employees work from home and keep in contact with the office using a computer and a modem. Write a report on the effects this way of working might have on the employee and the implications for the employer.   (20 marks)

(Edexcel, 1996 – H)

Shift systems

Computers do not need a break, they do not need to have a holiday, they will never become ill, they do not need to rest or sleep.

This means that the computer can work 24 hours a day, 365 days a year without a break. People are being asked to cover this time by working shifts, so instead of working 9.00am–5.00pm, they may be asked to work a rota. This rota could be broken down into three different shifts each of eight hours long. There are many other variations on shift-working.

Flexible working

In today's modern fast-paced environment, rigid hours of work are no longer suitable for many business needs. Many companies require their facilities to be functioning 24/7/365 – 24 hours a day, 7 days a week, 365 days a year – and to cater for this will require their employees to have flexible working. Companies can no longer afford to let equipment remain idle for long periods of the day/night.

As technology has taken a greater lead in many companies and computers/robots do not require any breaks, many jobs no longer require 9 till 5 working hours. A person who repairs or mends computers would have to be flexible because they will wait for a telephone call or message to say they are needed to repair a machine. This call could come during the evening, at weekends or bank holidays – whenever the computer breaks down. The company could not afford to let the computers stand idle for a great period of time, mainly because we have come to rely on them so much. If a machine is not working, then it is costing the company money and hindering somebody's work.

EQUIPMENT

Cost of installation

Computer equipment is very expensive to buy. If you buy a computer it is often said to be 'out of date' immediately you have bought it. Something new has already been introduced, which is better and more powerful than the original one purchased. This is because computers are continually being updated. The pace of change is very fast.

Therefore, companies will spend a great deal of time and energy in making sure that the computers they purchase are the correct ones for the jobs they need the machines to do. Computers are like cars, you always want the most up-to-date and modern one available. Once bought, you lose a great deal of money because they are classed as second-hand and the resale value is very low for second-hand computers.

Maintenance

Computers should never stand idle. If they are not working, they are losing the company money. Hence, technicians are employed whose job it is to ensure that the computers are functioning and working properly without any problems. Some of the problems could be software problems, other times it could be hardware. The technicians are given the task of ensuring that they are always working.

Upgrades

To keep pace with the fast-changing world in which we live, companies will always be updating their machines, if they do not then they could become uncompetitive – not being able to produce the same amount in a given time. This could lead to more unemployment. On a regular basis, companies will upgrade their machines. This means to replace the ones they already have with more efficient machines or machines that are capable of doing more jobs. The computer could be smaller but has greater memory facilities; or a much larger screen with reduced glare, therefore reducing health hazards etc.

Replacements

Many machines are replaced after they reach a certain age. Most companies make a decision that after a certain period of time there is a chance the computer will begin to have faults, through wear and tear of the day-to-day use etc. The company would rather pay out for new equipment as opposed to what could be expensive repair bills. Some companies even offer these computers for sale to their employees for home use to recoup some money back.

Profitability

Almost all companies are in business to make a profit. Therefore, it is imperative that the company has all its computers working properly and effectively. If the computers are not working, then they will not be making any money, which in turn reduces the profit that the company is making.

ENVIRONMENTAL ISSUES

Waste

The environment is extremely precious and it is important that wherever possible everyone tries to reduce the amount of waste they create. The use of e-mail has reduced the amount of paper that is used in the world, which in turn has reduced the number of trees that need to be cut down to produce the paper. Also the energy used to cut down the trees has also been saved, which could have an effect on global warming. This has become of great concern to business, the government and the public in recent years.

Most people are now concerned about the environment in which we live and how we protect what we have. There are many pressure groups who have helped in this process.

At the present time if a computer becomes out of date then it is normally upgraded by purchasing another one. The problem lies in what is being done with the old computer. There are issues here that have not yet been addressed by society but will have to be in the near future because the machines are not bio-degradable, adding to the problem we have of the disposal of certain items used in society.

Task *18.8*

List as many pressure groups as you can find. State exactly what each group is concerned about and how they go about keeping the public informed of what is happening.

There is a need to reduce wastage in industrial processes. There are many examples where computers have taken over the control and monitoring of different processes. For example, in the making of beer, the computer controls the temperature and this means that each barrel of beer is exactly the same as the last one produced – there can be no human error. Thus, the first barrel will taste the same as the last barrel. This cuts down on the amount of resources used in the process.

Recycling

Recycling the resources we have is becoming more and more important in modern life. Today, our society is considered as 'throw-away'. This means that all the goods we tend to purchase are packed in materials ready to be thrown away. This creates large quantities of waste material, which should be recycled. Many companies are aware of this as an environmental issue, together with the pressure from members of the public. The majority of the packaging we use today should be environmentally friendly i.e. it can be used again.

This 'throw-away' society creates huge amounts of litter in our towns and cities, which creates waste, which then has to be disposed of. The EU aims to convert all its members from throw-away to recycling societies in the next few years. To do this we must reuse such materials as paper, glass and steel cans. Hence the number of supermarkets and other local places having recycling facilities to encourage members of the public to be more environmentally friendly.

MARKET CONDITIONS

Competition

Competition keeps a number of companies in business. They have to compete with the next company to obtain their market share. They continually have to strive to improve their product or service so that they can survive in the business world. The car manufacturers are continually changing the designs of their cars to encourage people to buy them. The sole proprietor aims to improve his/her service so that they gain more customers than the shop further down the road. These are all means of trying to be competitive – being better than the other person or company.

Revision Questions

1 The skills of employees at Happy Ideas Ltd are improved by ....

pay   training   recruitment   selection

2 If no agreement is reached with employers, the members of a trade union may need to take ....

industrial action   profit-sharing   unlimited liability   contracts of employment

3 When the new automated ice-lolly plant was installed, employees could not operate it and needed to learn new ....

training   research   resources   skills

4 If Nocha Ltd needed to reduce the number of its employees, it could make some of them ....

redundant   work from home   reduce hours   earn less

5 Leroy Green, a self-employed plumber, ensures that all new employees have .... training.

on-the-job   off-the-job   induction   self-study

6 The Kendall's daughter had induction training ....

after 2 years   when starting her job   annually   off site

Task 18.9

The introduction of information technology at Happy Ideas Limited will not affect the production workers as all their work is done by hand. However, it will have an impact upon the office workers. Office workers will need training in the use of information technology.

1 What might be the effects of the introduction of information technology on the motivation of Happy Ideas Limited's workers?
(4 marks)

2 Explain TWO ways, other than training or motivation, that the introduction of information technology might affect Happy Ideas Ltd and its workers. (6 marks)

(Edexcel, 2000 – H)

Task 18.10

The Directors of Harbon Estates Ltd are planning to increase the use of information technology by all staff.

1 State TWO reasons why the Directors might wish to discuss this with staff. (2 marks)

2 Identify TWO problems that the Directors of Harbon Estates Ltd might have to deal with during the first few weeks of the changeover to using the new information technology.
(2 marks)

3 Explain TWO ways in which Harbon Estates Ltd might be more efficient when these problems have been solved.
(4 marks)

(Edexcel, 1998 – F)

Task 18.11

Many employers believe in increased co-operation with their employees and include them in the decision-making process. Employees, in return, must take responsibility for their actions and be flexible.

Assess the effect that this increased co-operation might have on employers and employees. (8 marks)

(Edexcel, 1998 – F)

Task 18.12

1 Petra Webster has just started at the Manchester showroom of Docdel plc as a mechanic. She will receive induction training. Explain ONE benefit she may receive from this training.
(3 marks)

2 Petra will also receive on-the-job training. Explain ONE benefit which this might bring to Docdel plc. (3 marks)

(Edexcel, 1997 – F)

Task 18.13

Many employers believe in increased co-operation with their employees and include them in the decision-making process. Employees, in return, must take responsibility for their actions and be flexible.

Assess the effect that this increased co-operation might have on employers and employees. (8 marks)

(Edexcel, 1998 – F)

Extension task

Docdel plc provides different types of training for its employees.

State the types of training and explain why each might be offered. (9 marks)

(Edexcel, 1998 – H)

xtension task

The Directors of Nocha Ltd are introducing information technology into the administration of the company.

1 What might the social effects be on employees as a result of this change? (6 marks)

2 What benefits might the introduction of information technology bring to Nocha Ltd? (6 marks)

In order to make this change effective, the Directors of Nocha Ltd will need to consider:

- training

- cost

- work patterns.

3 Select TWO of these and explain why each must be considered by the Directors. (8 marks)

(Edexcel, 1999 – F)

ASSESSMENT
COURSEWORK

Coursework is work that you do during your Business and Communication Systems course that, when it is marked, goes towards your final GCSE grade. The coursework element of Business and Communication Systems is worth 25% of the marks available at GCSE. It is compulsory – that means you have no choice and have to complete one piece of coursework.

WHAT IS GOOD ABOUT COURSEWORK?

- As you only have to complete one piece of coursework, you might as well try your hardest and get the best marks you can – do the best you can while you have the chance. Do not forget that your coursework goes towards your final grade so the best mark you can get means you do not have everything resting on your final examination mark. It gives you a psychological edge so you do not need to worry as much. The more you put in the more you get out!

- Coursework can be very enjoyable and give you a great sense of achievement when it is completed. It is probably the first major piece of work you will have completed on your own that is all yours and that is totally original.

- Coursework will make your work more interesting as you will be involved in activities that are different to ordinary classroom activities, for example, going out and doing some field research, interviewing people and perhaps working in groups. It is totally acceptable if you do research in a group but your coursework must be your own work and not the same as anyone else's.

■ You can show what you can do as it gives you the opportunity to use your skills. It also gives you the freedom to work at your own pace – within reason! You should be suitably proud of yourself when you have completed it.

So what is a coursework assignment?

Four coursework assignments are provided by the examination board, Edexcel, and are linked to the four sections of the specification as follows:

1 Communication systems

2 Data gathering, recording and presentation systems

3 Money transfer systems

4 Constraints and influences on systems.

Each piece of coursework sets you a problem to investigate. You will need to prepare an action plan that helps you plan how you are going to tackle your coursework. You will set yourself tasks and deadlines, as well as looking at the various books and resources you might use. An action plan sheet is provided in this unit, which might help you with your planning.

You will be required to carry out some research and collect data. Some research you will do in the classroom using textbooks, notes and possibly the Internet. Other research can be collected using questionnaires or surveys or through interviews.

Once this data has been collected, you will analyse your findings and form some conclusions and possibly make recommendations.

You should word process your report and include tables, charts, graphs and illustrations, which will make it easier for the reader to follow and understand, as well as make your report look more interesting. But make sure you refer to any charts and graphs in your text and that they are relevant to the coursework.

You can use the following headings to present your report:

■ Introduction – which will include the purpose of the report

■ Research – describe your research methods

■ Findings – what did you find out?

■ Conclusions

■ Recommendations and any implications.

How is the coursework marked?

Your coursework is marked out of 36 and these marks are recorded on a **Record Sheet**, which is included in this unit for your reference. When you first see this you will probably find it very confusing but one of the keys to success with coursework is understanding the Record Sheet and the assessment criteria.

You will want to get as many of the tick boxes as you can ticked so the following guidance will hopefully help you do this.

ASSESSMENT CRITERIA

1. DEMONSTRATE knowledge and understanding of the specified subject

1.1 Demonstrate basic knowledge or identify basic factors
Have you shown basic knowledge about any area of the syllabus? For example, what is a local area network?

1.2 Identify sources of knowledge – text/people/organisations, electronic – any 2 sources
Where did you get your knowledge? If you interviewed someone, name that person. Include the title and author of any textbooks. State any web addresses you used and name any organisations you used.

1.3 Identify purposes of a system
Have you stated at least two purposes? For example, the purpose of the network is to improve the efficiency and speed of communication.

1.4 Recognise constraints
Are there any constraints? For example, the computer cannot be used because staff are not trained. Remember to include more than one constraint.

1.5 Recognise differences
Have you shown that you recognise differences? For example, what is the difference between a standing order and a direct debit?

1.6 Consider influences
Have you thought about what influences decisions? For example, whether to purchase a desk jet or a laser printer or whether to use a written memo or the telephone. Remember to include more than one influence.

1.7 Consider alternatives
Have you considered more than one thing? For example, different methods of communication or different work patterns.

1.8 Show sound knowledge and understanding
Have you shown that you understand? For example, by writing in detail.

1.9 Make critical comparisons
Have you shown that you understand? For example, by writing in detail.

2. APPLY knowledge and understanding using appropriate terms, concepts, theories and methods

2.1 State basic terms or concepts or theories
Have you used specialist terms? For example, a business has the option to use electronic forms of communication like e-mail.

2.2 Apply basic methods
Have you used methods? For example, did you use a questionnaire to collect data? This is one method, another method might be using a spreadsheet.

2.3 Prepare basic action plan
Have you used the action plan sheet to plan your work?

2.4 Consider issues or legislation
Have you thought about any issues? For example, Health and Safety or training or Data Protection and how these might affect the organisation.

2.5 Apply methods relevant to topic
Have you used any relevant methods? For example, using a database to record employee details or a flow chart to illustrate a process.

2.6 Develop action plan
Have you added any dates or modifications to your action plan?

2.7 Recognise strengths and limitations of ideas used and make decisions
Have you included the strengths and limitations or advantages and disadvantages of something and THEN made decisions? For example, the advantages and disadvantages of video-conferencing and then reasons for any decisions you make as to whether to use this or not.

2.8 Effectively address topic
Have you completed a thorough piece of work and included all you can?

2.9 Present action plan
Have you included a really thorough action plan, with all dates, modifications and changes included, which reflects the way you completed your coursework?

3. SELECT, organise, analyse and interpret information from various sources to analyse problems and issues

3.1 Gather basic information
Have you gathered any information? For example, any data collected from your research.

3.2 Record information
Have you recorded any information? For example, using text, graphs, charts, application form.

3.3 Collate information
Have you put your coursework into a sensible order with page numbers and a contents page?

3.4 Gather additional informtion from a minimum of three sources or show some ability to organise and use
Have you used three sources of information or have you shown you can use software, for example, to produce graphs/charts and insert these into text?

3.5 Review or interpret information
Have you considered your findings? For example, what does your data tell you – that 75% of companies used a fax machine?

3.6 Consider alternatives
Have you thought about different ways of collecting information? For example, desk/field research. Or have you considered different ways of presenting information? For example, pie charts or bar charts.

3.7 Organise a systematic gathering of information from four sources
Have you used all four sources to collect your data and information and can you prove this?

3.8 Apply information to task and use effectively
Have you analysed your data and any other information you have collected and is it relevant to your original task?

3.9 Prepare a logical and comprehensive report or presentation
Have you prepared a thorough and full report, using report format with an introduction, research methods, findings and analysis, recommendations and possibly implications?

4. EVALUATE evidence, make reasoned judgements and present conclusions accurately and appropriately

4.1 Make basic comments
Have you stated any conclusions? For example, I recommend using post only for sending bulky documents, because e-mail is so much quicker.

4.2 Relate conclusions to task
Have you stated your original task and then related your conclusions to this? For example, the new network is good because it will increase efficiency and make communication quicker.

4.3 Make basic reference to financial or social or environmental effects
Have you made any reference to any of the above? For example, I would recommend training even though it will cost money because it will ensure all employees are both confident and able when using computers.

4.4 Consider results or make limited attempt at analysis and conclusion
Have you looked at your findings and made any conclusions? For example, as 90% of companies surveyed used e-mail and it is being used more and more for both internal and external communication, I am recommending introducing this to the company.

4.5 Draw limited conclusions and make a recommendation
Have you made any recommendations? For example, I recommend a LAN so large computer files can be transferred quickly, everyone has access to data and files, and better printers can be bought.

4.6 Consider financial or social or environmental effects
Have you thought about any of the above effects? For example, the company should use video-conferencing because it allows face-to-face meetings without having to leave the office environment. This, in turn, will save time and money spent on travel.

4.7 Evaluate outcomes and indicate possible improvements
Have you looked at any outcomes and thought about improvements? For example, the result of interviewing staff showed that they wanted more training so introducing a regular training programme (outcome) should result in an increase in confidence using the network (improvement) and less mistakes being made (improvement). You would need to include another outcome to gain this criteria.

4.8 Produce a detailed evaluation, suggest and justify relevant improvements
Does your report contain a thorough evaluation of the problem and have you suggested any recommendations or improvements? In order to justify your recommendation include the benefits that they will bring.

4.9 Link financial or social or environmental effects to suggestions
What effects will your suggestions have on the organisation etc? For example, I would recommend the company invest in new systems (suggestion) because jobs will get completed quicker and more efficiently resulting in time saved (financial effect). If clients can find more out about the company on the Internet they will gain more interest and more sales (another financial effect).

ACTION PLAN

TIME/DATE/ BY WHEN	WHAT I INTEND TO DO	RESOURCES	PROBLEMS/ADJUSTMENTS

GCSE BUSINESS AND COMMUNICATION SYSTEMS 1504 RECORD SHEET

Candidate Name: Candidate No: Centre Name: Centre No:

1. DEMONSTRATE knowledge and understanding of the specified subject content (Each ticked box is equal to ONE mark)

1.1 Demonstrate basic knowledge or identify basic factors	1.4 Recognise constraints
1.2 Identify sources of knowledge – text, people, organisations, electronic – any 2	1.5 Recognise differences
1.3 Identify purposes of a system	1.6 Consider influences
	1.7 Consider alternatives
	1.8 Show sound knowledge and understanding
	1.9 Make critical comparisons

2. APPLY knowledge and understanding using appropriate terms, concepts, theories and methods effectively to address problems and issues (Each ticked box is equal to ONE mark)

2.1 State basic terms or concepts or theories	2.4 Consider issues or legislation
2.2 Apply basic methods	2.5 Apply methods relevant to topic
2.3 Prepare basic action plan	2.6 Develop action plan
	2.7 Recognise strengths and limitations of ideas used and make decisions
	2.8 Effectively address topic
	2.9 Present action plan

3. SELECT, organise and analyse and interpret information from various sources to analyse problems and issues (Each ticked box is equal to ONE mark)

3.1 Gather basic information	3.4 Gather additional information from a minimum of 3 sources or show some ability to organise and use
3.2 Record information	3.5 Review or interpret information
3.3 Collate information	3.6 Consider alternatives
	3.7 Organise a systematic gathering of information from 4 sources
	3.8 Apply information to task and use effectively
	3.9 Prepare a logical and comprehensive report or presentation

4. EVALUATE EVIDENCE, make reasoned judgements and present conclusions accurately and appropriately (Each ticked box is equal to ONE mark)

4.1 Make basic comments	4.4 Consider results or make limited attempt at analysis and conclusion
4.2 Relate conclusions to task	4.5 Draw limited conclusions and make a recommendation
4.3 Make basic reference to financial or social or environmental effects	4.6 Consider financial or social or environmental effects
	4.7 Evaluate outcomes and indicate possible improvements
	4.8 Produce a detailed evaluation, suggest and justify relevant improvements
	4.9 Link financial or social or environmental effects to suggestions

NB Candidates may score at any point but Teacher Examiners and Moderators must be satisfied that the candidate is generally meeting the level indicated.
Scripts must be annotated with criteria codes and this Record Sheet attached to scripts.

Marks out of 36   × 2   +QWC/4   = Total Mark (to be transferred to OPTEMS)

TOTAL (Max 36)

THE EXAMINATION PAPERS

You have completed your coursework and got a good mark, now you can start thinking about the exams. There are two exam papers in this subject consisting of:

■ Paper 1 – a practical paper consisting of 3 questions and lasting 1½ hours

■ Paper 2 – a written theory paper also consisting of 3 questions and lasting 1 hour.

As with most examinations, there are 2 tiers:

■ Foundation Tier – grades C – G

■ Higher Tier – grades A* – D.

Which tier you take will depend on how you have done throughout the year with classwork, homework and your coursework. You and your teacher will decide this during year 11.

Each examination series is based upon a scenario that is based on a real company. You can see the scenario during year 11 in order that you can prepare thoroughly for your final exams. The scenario is included as the first page of your exams so it is the first thing you see when you open the papers.

The following are examples of specimen questions:

PAPER 1 – FOUNDATION PRACTICAL EXAM

The owners of 'Teddies on the Circle' have decided to produce an A4 leaflet for customers. One of the owners has made a note of some ideas. His notes are shown below.

ADDRESS: 2 Factory Lane, Stoneybridge, SB47 8BR

Available from March 2001

Can be ordered from many shops

Graphic could be used

TEL 01952 339741

EMAIL TOC@aol.com

Use suitable software to design the notice to fill one side of A4 paper.

Your notice should include:

- different font sizes
- different fonts.

(15 marks)

PAPER 2 – HIGHER PRACTICAL EXAM

The shop manager at 'Teddies on the Circle' has asked you to design a leaflet for customers. His rough notes are shown below.

size 12 cm x 16 cm

two appropriate graphics

three types of emphasis

Content:

Name of shop emphasised and centred
Graphic of bear at top
Large shop
1000 of bears
Open daily 10-6
Telephone 01952 334942
Address – 3 The Crescent, Stoneybridge SB4 9TR
E-mail address – Teddies@aol.com
NB Address/tel no and e-mail at bottom – address first
Things we offer – mail order, all credit cards, teddy gifts, deposit on a bear secures.

Use suitable software to design the advertisement within the dimensions indicated.

(15 marks)

PAPER 3 – FOUNDATION THEORY EXAM

1 When bears are received at 'Teddies on the Circle' they are
checked against . . .

a receipt   a cheque   a credit note   a delivery note

2 The manager needs to communicate with employees. He could
use a notice or hold a meeting. Which method would you
recommend and why?   (6 marks)

3 The company has to communicate with:

   ▪ customers

   ▪ suppliers

   Compare different methods of communication that might be
   used.   (6 marks)

PAPER 4 – HIGHER THEORY EXAM

1 The following software:

   ▪ database

   ▪ spreadsheet

   ▪ desktop publishing

   is used in the running of the Collectors Club. Assess the benefits
   of using this software.   (12 marks)

2 The managers have extended the duties of Paula Jones to include
   responsibility for the security of data and files due to some
   problems that have occurred lately:

   ▪ an e-mail containing a virus

   ▪ private files being opened by people other than the owner of the files.

   Suggest recommendations that Paula should make to the
   Systems Manager for improving security.   (10 marks)

SOME EXAM ADVICE

▪ Use a black or blue pen. Do not use a pencil. This can make your examination
script difficult to read, which means the examiner might miss something you
have written that is worth marks. Do not throw marks away unnecessarily!

■ Candidates lose marks because they do not do exactly what the examiner wants. Therefore make sure that you read the questions properly – answer the question as it is written and not how you want it to be!

■ If the question asks for TWO reasons, make sure you only give two reasons, not one or three.

■ Here are some key words used in exam questions:

  ■ identify/state/list – usually only requires one-word answers

  ■ explain/outline – make a point and develop it

  ■ discuss/compare – explain two sides of a point – advantages and disadvantages

  ■ assess – make a point, develop it and start to make conclusions

  ■ evaluate – after discussion and analysis, make judgement(s).

■ There are lines on the paper for your answer – the examiner will expect to see these lines filled.

■ Be aware of the marks allocated to each question – make sure you give enough in your answer to gain maximum marks.

■ Do not answer in statements (unless the question asks for a list of statements). Always try and expand on your answer. For example, *a LAN is a local area network* (this is a statement) *which means computers are linked together usually through a cable and can share printers and programs* (this is an expanded answer).

■ Try and use words like *because, therefore, so* to link statements and expansions/explanations together.

■ In questions that call for extended writing, you are advised to use some sort of plan – this can be a spidergram or a list of points – because this leads to well-structured arguments. This approach helps you to organise your thoughts, which means that you will not repeat yourself and you will produce a well-planned answer.

■ In the practical exam, remember to label all printouts with your name, candidate number, centre number and question number.

Finally, do enjoy the exams. If you do your best it's all anyone can ask.

Good Luck!

GLOSSARY

A

access – entry to programs or networks

action plan – a list of tasks with dates intended to be done

agenda – a list of items to be discussed at a meeting

B

BACS (Bankers Automated Clearing System) – payment made by electronic transfer between bank computers

body language – unspoken messages and signals

bonus – money given in addition to a wage

buyer – a person who buys something

C

catalogue – booklet containing a list of items

cell – a box in a spreadsheet

chain of command – the path in an organisation along which decisions/orders pass

cheque – an order for a bank to pay money

commission – a fee paid for achieving something eg sales target

communication – the sending and receiving of information

credit card – a card provided by a bank which allows the holder to obtain goods on credit (not paying cash for them)

credit note – given to a buyer in order to reduce the amount owing because goods are damaged

D

data – usually factual information

database – a structured collection of data

data capture sheet – used to collect data before input into the computer

Data Protection Act – an Act of Parliament which controls the use and storage of personal data

debit card – used to pay for goods instead of using cash

debit note – a document charging for any additional products supplied

delegation – acting on behalf of someone else

delivery note – sent with ordered goods as proof of receipt

direct debit – an order to collect money from another person's bank account

E

e-commerce (electronic commerce) – the sale and purchase of goods via the Internet

EDI (electronic data interchange) – two businesses can order goods from one another without all the paperwork

EFTPOS (electronic funds transfer at point of sale) – when goods are paid for by bank card and passed through a reader attached to the point of sale terminal (till) – the money is taken directly from the customer's bank

e-mail (electronic mail) – messages sent from computer user to computer user

F

face-to-face – speaking to someone personally – usually a meeting

facsimile machine (fax) – a machine which can send a copy of a document via a telephone link

field – a data item in a record of a database

file – a collection of records in a database

flexitime – employees working hours to suit them, within limits

flowchart – a diagram which shows the flow of information through a system

font – the size and style of a typeface eg Times New Roman

formula – a set of numbers in a spreadsheet

fully-blocked – all lines at the left hand margin are aligned

G

grapevine – an unofficial channel of communication – how rumours are spread

graphics – drawings, charts, images

H

hacker – someone who gets access to a computer system illegally

hierarchy – the vertical structure of an organisation

I

ice-breaker – an activity that enables people to get to know each other

import – when data created in one application (maybe a spreadsheet) is brought into another application (maybe a word processing document)

income tax – tax paid as a proportion of pay

information – is knowledge gained from investigation

ISP (Internet Service Provider) – an organisation which provides access to the Internet eg AOL, Demon

Inland Revenue – UK government department responsible for the assessment and collection of tax

input – enter data into a computer eg via a keyboard

Internet – a worldwide network

Internet banking – being able to operate a bank account using the Internet

interview – a formal meeting to assess a person's suitability for a job

intranet – a network of computers based in one building or organisation

itinerary – a route or list of places to visit

invoice – a list of goods and prices

J

justification – aligning text at the left, right or both margins

L

LAN – see local area network

layout – the arrangement of text, images etc on a page

letter – formal method of communication

local area network – computers on one site which are linked by cables and which share resources

M

magnetic ink character recognition – data printed in special ink eg details on a cheque

meeting – a coming together of people

memorandum – an internal method of communication

minutes – a record of items discussed at a meeting together with any decisions made

MICR – see magnetic ink character recognition

modem – allows two computers to communicate using a telephone line

N

National Insurance – payments deducted from a salary which are used to provide benefits and pensions

network – see LAN and WAN

newsletter – a printed report that gives information which is of interest to members of clubs eg Computer Club

NI – see National Insurance

notice of meeting – details of a future meeting – time, date, venue

O

open punctuation – in letters when punctuation only appears in the body of the letter

operating system – a program which manages all the resources of a computer system

oral communication – spoken

order form – a form used to request goods

organisation chart – the internal structure of a business

output – any data coming from a computer whether printed, displayed on screen, sent to another computer or saved

overtime – time worked over the total number of normal working hours

P

pager – a device that sends a simple message to someone

password – a word which is entered with a user ID in order to get into a computer system, used to restrict access

PAYE (Pay As You Earn) – a scheme used for collecting income tax from pay

payslip – details of pay and any deductions from pay

personal data – someone's personal details

piece rate – payment based on output

presentation – something that is presented eg a talk to a group of people

public messaging system – an electronic noticeboard

Q

query – used to retrieve information from a database

questionnaire – a list of questions used to collect data

quotation – the price and terms of goods/services a business charges

R

record – a collection of data in a database

remittance advice – a document sent by a buyer to a seller stating that payment is being made

report – output from a database or a written account of something eg some research

S

salary – pay, usually based on 12 equal monthly payments

schedule – a timetable of events

search – to look for information in a database

seller – a person selling something

sort – change the order of records in a database or lines in a spreadsheet

span of control – the number of workers one person directly controls

spreadsheet – a grid of cells used for calculations

standing order – an instruction to a bank to make regular payments to someone

statement of account – contains details of all transactions between a seller and a buyer and sent to the buyer at the end of each month

style sheet – another word for a template

T

table – how statistical data is presented in columns and rows

telebanking – being able to operate a bank account over the telephone

template – used in word processing and DTP as a framework which can be saved

time rate – payment based on hours worked

U

user ID (user identification) – the name of a user of a computer

V

video conferencing – people in different places can hold meetings where no one has to travel yet everyone can see each other

W

WAN – see wide area network

wage – pay given to workers usually weekly

white space – the space left on a page after text, images, tables, charts etc have been placed

wide area network – WAN – computers linked over a wide geographical area

INDEX